Golden Shores

Travel Guide To

TRIESTE

ITALY

EDEN CHOICE

Copyright & Disclaimer

All rights reserved. No part of this book may be reproduced or used in any form without the publisher's written permission, except for brief quotations in a book review.

Please note that the information contained within this document is for educational purposes only. The information contained herein has been obtained from sources believed to be reliable at the time of publication. The opinions expressed herein are subject to change without notice.

Readers acknowledge that the Author / Publisher is not engaging in rendering legal, financial or professional advice. The Publisher / Author disclaims all warranties as to the accuracy, completeness, or adequacy of such information.

The Publisher assumes no liability for errors, omissions, or inadequacies in the information contained herein or from the interpretations thereof. The publisher / Author specifically disclaims any liability from the use or application of the information contained herein or from the interpretations thereof.

Dedicated To:

_____

This book is dedicated to all wayfaring folks, those who love the spirit of adventure, and those who take traveling as both education and fun.

❝

Trieste, a windswept jewel where Central Europe meets the Adriatic, invites travelers to wander through grand cafés, sunlit plazas, and echoes of empires past.

Here, the soul finds its rhythm in sea breezes, slow sips of coffee, and stories written in stone.

Table of Contents

Copyright
Dedication
Quotes

09 **Introduction - Welcome to Trieste, Italy**
Trieste welcomes you with a unique blend of cultures, where Roman ruins meet Habsburg elegance and Slavic charm. This guide is your key to exploring its history, cuisine, nature, and soul like a well-connected local.

15 **Chapter One - How to get to Trieste.**
Whether by plane, train, bus, or ferry, Trieste is remarkably well-connected and easy to reach. Its location at the crossroads of Italy, Slovenia, and the Adriatic makes the journey part of the experience.

21 **Chapter Two - Best Time to Visit and Length of Stay**
From spring blooms to fall sailing regattas, every season in Trieste brings a new charm. Whether you're staying for a weekend or a week, there's always something worth discovering.

29 **Chapter Three - Top ten tourist attractions in Trieste**
Trieste dazzles with its seaside squares, imperial castles, and ancient ruins tucked into city hills. From the grandeur of Miramare Castle to the mystery of Roman theatres, every corner holds a story.

47 **Chapter Four - Where to Stay: Accommodation in Trieste**
Whether you dream of luxury by the sea or a cozy guesthouse in Old Town, Trieste has a stay that suits you. Unique finds like floating hotels and vineyard retreats add extra magic.

Table of Contents

59   **Chapter Five - Trieste for Foodies—Where and What to Eat**

Trieste's cuisine is a love letter to its crossroads—where Italian, Slavic, and Austrian flavors dance on every plate. From rich jota to sweet fritole, every bite tells a story.

67   **Chapter Six - Transportation in Trieste**

Getting around Trieste is easy and scenic, whether by tram, ferry, or on foot along the waterfront. Day trips by car or boat open up a world of coastal beauty.

71   **Chapter Seven - Practical Tips for Your Stay**

With a little local know-how—like currency, safety, and language basics—your stay will be smooth and stress-free. This chapter gives you the essentials for blending in and feeling at home.

75   **Chapter Eight - Do's and Don'ts of Trieste**

Respecting cultural etiquette and avoiding tourist pitfalls helps you travel smarter and deeper. Learn the unspoken rules, from coffee customs to local laws.

81   **Chapter Nine - Itineraries for All Travelers**

Whether you're a solo adventurer, a family planner, or a couple chasing sunsets, there's a tailored plan for you. These itineraries make the most of every moment.

97   **Chapter Ten - Trieste on a Budget**

Enjoy Trieste's charm without splurging—thanks to free museums, seaside walks, and street food delights. Budget travel here still feels rich with experience.

Table of Contents

103   **Chapter Eleven - Exploring Trieste's surroundings**
Trieste is the perfect base for discovering Slovenia, Croatia, and the Karst region's hidden vineyards and castles. Just a short ride brings you to new worlds.

109   **Chapter Twelve - Art and Culture in Trieste**
The city's artistic soul shines in its theatres, galleries, and literary cafés. Trieste's heritage inspired the likes of Joyce and Svevo—and it might just stir your own muse too.

115   **Chapter Thirteen - Nightlife in Trieste**
From elegant wine bars to lively live music by the sea, the city glows after dark. A sunset stroll or jazz set becomes the perfect ending to your day.

121   **Chapter Fourteen - Shopping in Trieste**
Browse stylish boutiques, artisan markets, and gourmet shops full of local flavor. Whether you're hunting for vintage treasures or handmade souvenirs, shopping here feels like a slow, stylish stroll.

125   **Chapter Fifteen - Trieste For Nature Lovers**
Nature thrives just beyond the piazzas, from coastal trails to forested cliffs. Hike, bike, or birdwatch your way into Trieste's wild, peaceful side.

131   **Chapter Sixteen - Plan Your Visit to the Beach**
Trieste's coastline is dotted with pebbled coves, beach clubs, and spots to dive into the Adriatic blue. Each beach has its own rhythm—from hidden escapes to lively shores.

Table of Contents

137   **Chapter Seventeen - Family-friendly Activities**
Trieste welcomes families with museums, parks, and kid-friendly beaches perfect for play and learning. Day trips and guided tours make it easy to keep everyone smiling.

143   **Chapter Eighteen - Romantic Activities to Do in Trieste**
Couples can stroll sunset piers, dine under starlight, or relax in serene spas. Trieste turns ordinary moments into memories laced with charm.

149   **Chapter Nineteen - Hidden Gems of Trieste**
Beyond the main sights, Trieste hides secret cafés, quiet viewpoints, and stories waiting in silent alleys. These lesser-known wonders give your trip a personal touch.

155   **Chapter Twenty - Practical Advice for Longer Stays**
If you're staying longer, this chapter helps you live like a local—from renting apartments to navigating paperwork and meeting the expat community. Settle in, and let Trieste feel like home.

161   Appendix
Maps
Accreditations
My Other Books

INTRODUCTION

Welcome to Trieste, Italy

Welcome to Trieste, a hidden treasure along Italy's northeastern coast! Perched between the azure waves of the Adriatic Sea and the rocky limestone cliffs of the Carso Plateau, this lovely city combines history, culture, and nature.

Despite being eclipsed by more prominent Italian towns such as Rome, Venice, and Florence, Trieste has a certain charm of its own.

The city's rich history, formed by Roman, Austrian, and Slavic influences, can be seen everywhere, from the towering grandeur of Piazza Unità d'Italia to the charming lanes that weave through the Old Town.

First-time visitors to Trieste may be surprised.

Its historical significance as a major port city of the Austro-Hungarian Empire, along with its closeness to Slovenia, lends it an international air.

This city feels distinct from the rest of Italy, which is exactly what makes it so unique.

Whether you are visiting for a weekend or planning a longer stay, Trieste's diverse cultures, cuisine, and breathtaking scenery will enchant you.

About the Travel Guide

Traveling may be thrilling, but the sheer volume of information can make preparation seem daunting.

That is where this guide comes in. I created this Trieste travel guide with one single goal in mind: to make your trip as seamless and pleasurable as possible.

Whether you are a first-time tourist, a seasoned traveler visiting Italy, or a returning visitor to Trieste, this guide will help you discover the best of the city's offerings.

This handbook includes the following information:

Curated Information: Discover top tourist sites, local restaurants, and hidden gems only locals know.

There is no need to sift through innumerable blogs or reviews. Everything here has been selected for its quality and authenticity.

Itineraries for all types of travelers: We have itineraries to suit every sort of tourist, whether you are a solitary traveler, a couple on a romantic break, or a family with children.

There is no one-size-fits-all solution here.
Each traveler has unique interests and demands, and we have taken those into account to make your vacation more personalized and stress-free.

Practical Tips: Learn when to travel, how to get there, where to stay, how to use public transit, and avoid tourist traps.

There is also a chapter on what to do —and what not to do—to make your vacation as authentic as possible.

Appendix includes addresses for popular motels, eateries, and emergency contacts.
You will not have to spend time Googling or figuring out how to go to your next location.

This book is intended to be your go-to resource, whether you are wandering for a few days or settling in for a week of adventure.

By the end of the book, you will feel as if you already knew Trieste inside and out, and you will be confident in exploring its streets.

Why Trieste, Italy?

Now you may be wondering, "Why Trieste?" With so many well-known sites in Italy, why should you spend time in an off-the-beaten-path city?
Here's why Trieste is a must-see, whether you are visiting for the first time or coming back for more:

A Crossroads of Culture
Trieste lies at a unique cultural crossroads. It was formerly the principal port of the Austro-Hungarian Empire, therefore its architecture, cafés, and even gastronomy are heavily influenced by Viennese culture.
Add to that its closeness to Slovenia and Croatia, and you get a city that combines Mediterranean, Central European, and Balkan influences.
Strolling around Trieste is like strolling across several periods of European history in one location.

A Roman amphitheater, Habsburg-era palaces, and Slavic-influenced districts are all within a few kilometers of one another.

The Coffee Culture.
Trieste has a long and deep history with coffee. In fact, it is regarded as Italy's coffee capital! It was formerly the primary hub for coffee commerce and imports under the Austrian Empire, and this love of the bean has endured.
Café culture is serious business here, with famous cafés like Caffè San Marco serving as not only a location to have a cappuccino, but also a site for intellectual and literary discussions.

James Joyce even spent many years in Trieste!
Whether you are a casual coffee consumer or a coffee expert, you will like the café environment here.

Stunning architecture and views
You will be hard pushed to discover a city with more breathtaking panoramic vistas. The city's beachfront spans along the Adriatic Sea, offering visitors breathtaking sunsets and pleasant walks.

Piazza Unità d'Italia, the city's main central plaza, is one of Europe's largest and opens immediately into the sea.

You should also visit the neighboring Miramare Castle, a 19th-century castle with a view of the ocean.
On a clear day, the mountaintop San Giusto Castle offers panoramic views over the city, the sea, and Slovenia.

Perfect for day trips.
Trieste's position gives it an ideal base for visiting the surrounding regions.
Do you want to visit Slovenia for the day? It is about a 30 minute drive.

Croatia's gorgeous beaches are less than two hours away.
Even Venice is just a short train ride away! If you wish to venture outside of the city, Trieste has easy access to numerous nations as well as some of Europe's most stunning coastline roads.

Outdoor activities.
Do you love nature? Trieste is ideal for outdoor enthusiasts.
If you enjoy being active, there are several activities available, including trekking in the adjacent Val Rosandra Nature Reserve and sailing along the Adriatic coast.

The Carso Plateau's limestone cliffs are great for rock climbing, and if you are feeling daring, you may also explore underwater tunnels.

Rich Literary and Artistic Heritage
Trieste is more than simply a lovely city; it has inspired many of the world's finest writers. Trieste was formerly home to James Joyce, Italo Svevo, and Umberto Saba, and the city has served as the setting for several literary works.

If you enjoy reading, Trieste's bookstores, museums, and literary icons will excite you.
In a nutshell, Trieste provides the ideal balance of history, culture, environment, and modern amenities. It is a city that is simple to adore and even easier to discover.

How To Use This Guide
Planning a trip to a new city may be daunting, especially when there is so much to see and do.
That is why this book has been designed to be simple to use, whether you are planning your trip ahead of time or need a fast reference while on the road.

Here's how to make the most of it:

Determine what suits your travel style.
One of the most appealing aspects of this book is that it appeals to a variety of tourists.
You may be a budget-conscious backpacker, a couple searching for a romantic vacation, or a family traveling with children.

Whatever your travel style, we have put up personalized itineraries and advice to help you make the most of your stay in Trieste.
Turn to the "Itineraries for Every Traveler" chapter for options tailored to your specific travel tastes.

Use it for pre-trip planning.
This guide will help you plan your vacation to Trieste before you ever arrive.
Want to know when is the ideal time to visit?
Check out the weather and events sections if you want to schedule your vacation around festivals or favorable seasons.

Curious about where to stay?
The lodging chapter will go over the greatest possibilities, ranging from low-cost hotels to upscale boutique stays.
You will get booking hints and practical advise on the region of the city to stay in according on your requirements.

13

Explore day by day or at your own pace
If you are the type of traveler who enjoys planning every minute of your vacation, utilize the thorough itineraries in this guide to help you manage your days.
We have included ideas for weekend getaways, family vacations, and more. However, if you prefer a more relaxed approach, the instruction is still valuable.

Skip forward to the "Top Attractions" chapter and prepare a brief list of what interests you.
Then, explore Trieste at your own leisure, doing what seems appropriate for you that day.

Keep it Handy for On-the-Go Advice
While touring Trieste, this guide will be your best buddy.
Do you need a restaurant recommendation for lunch?
Check the cuisine area for the top local restaurants. Looking for transportation tips?

The guide will help you easily navigate buses, trams, and taxis. We have also included advice on avoiding frequent tourist blunders and traveling like a native, so you may have a smooth trip.

Make Use Of The Appendix
The appendix is rich with useful information.
You will discover emergency numbers, locations for the top hotels, restaurants, and pubs, as well as local words to assist you navigate about.

Keep this area bookmarked—it is a wonderful quick reference for important information you may need throughout your journey.

Return for your next trip.
Finally, do not see this tutorial as a one-time use resource.
Trieste is a city with a rich history and culture that would require several visits to properly understand.
Keep this information available for future visits; you could discover a whole new aspect of the city the next time you visit.

So there you have it.
This Trieste travel guide is your ultimate resource for experiencing the city like a native while also visiting all of the must-see attractions.
Whether it is your first visit or your tenth, Trieste has something for everyone, and this guide will help you depart with unforgettable memories.

CHAPTER 1

How to Get to Trieste

Trieste, in northern Italy, has a rich cultural heritage and stunning views.
This magnificent place may be reached in a variety of ways due to its unusual location along the Adriatic Sea and closeness to the borders of Slovenia and Croatia.

Whether you want to fly, ride the train, or go by boat, arriving to Trieste is an adventure in and of itself.
Let us have a look at the best methods to get to this attractive city, beginning with air travel and progressing through the numerous means of transportation available.

Flying To Trieste: Airports And Airlines

If you are flying into Trieste, the most convenient entrance point is Trieste - Friuli Venezia Giulia Airport (TRS), sometimes known as Trieste Airport.

The airport is about 33 kilometers (20 miles) northwest of the city, in the village of Ronchi dei Legionari.

It is a tiny but efficient airport with direct flights to and from numerous major European cities, making it a convenient destination for both local and international passengers.

Airlines Serving Trieste

Trieste Airport is served by a number of airlines, including both full-service and low-cost carriers, so you should be able to find a trip that fits your budget. Some of the major airlines operating here are:

Lufthansa connects from Munich, a key hub, with flights to locations worldwide.
Alitalia (ITA Airways) offers a convenient connection between Trieste and Rome, making it ideal for anyone going to or from Italy's capital.
Ryanair offers affordable flights from cities such as London, Valencia, and other European locations.

Volotea offers regional flights from cities including Naples, Catania, and Palermo.
During the summer, the airport usually enhances its offers with seasonal flights to famous tourist locations around Europe.

Traveling from Trieste Airport to the City Center
Once you have arrived, getting from the airport to the city center is simple. There are various solutions to fit any travel style:

Regular airport shuttle service connects Trieste Airport to the city bus and rail station (Trieste Centrale).
The travel lasts around 40 minutes, and tickets may be purchased at the airport or online.

Taxis are available at the airport, with fares to the city center ranging from €50 to €70.
The trip normally takes around 30 minutes, depending on traffic.
Major automobile rental firms, including Hertz, Europcar, and Avis, offer airport counters for those who prefer to bring their own vehicle.

Arrive via train: Trieste Centrale
For those traveling throughout Europe, arriving in Trieste by rail is a convenient and picturesque choice.
Trieste Centrale, the city's major rail station, is located in the center of the city, just a short walk from popular tourist destinations including Piazza Unità d'Italia and the seaside.

Trieste is well connected to Italy's national train network, as well as international lines that reach neighboring Slovenia and Austria.

Domestic train routes to Trieste
Travelers from different regions of Italy often take the Venice to Trieste rail route.

The travel takes around 2 hours by regional rail (Regionale Veloce) and is an excellent opportunity to explore northern Italy's gorgeous countryside.

There are also high-speed trains (Frecciabianca) that take around an hour and 30 minutes to make the trip.

The rail route from Milan to Trieste takes around 4 to 5 hours, but it is an effective method to get through northern Italy without flying.

International train routes
Ljubljana to Trieste: Trieste is less than a hundred kilometers from Slovenia's capital, Ljubljana.

A direct rail service connects the two cities, with a trip time of around 2 hours.
This is a great choice if you want to see both Italy and Slovenia.

Vienna to Trieste is a popular international route from Vienna.

ÖBB (Austrian Railways) operates high-speed trains from Vienna to Trieste in around 8 hours, providing comfortable seats and spectacular views of the Austrian Alps and rolling landscapes of northern Italy.

> "The gladdest moment in human life is a departure into unknown lands."
>
> — Sir Richard Burton

Local transportation from Trieste Centrale

Once you arrive at Trieste Centrale, the city's public transportation system makes it simple to get to your hotel or explore the area.
Bus routes connect the station to all sections of the city, and taxis are widely accessible outside.
If you prefer to walk, the ancient city center is about 10-15 minutes away.

Routes And Bus Connections
For those who appreciate the freedom of the open road, traveling to Trieste is an excellent opportunity to explore the surrounding areas.

The city is well-connected by roads, and its proximity to Italy's borders with Slovenia and Croatia makes it a popular stop on road journeys across southern Europe.

Driving to Trieste.
From Venice: Drive to Trieste in roughly 2 hours along the A4 highway. The path is easy, and you will pass through some gorgeous terrain along the way.
The trip from Ljubljana, Slovenia's capital, is picturesque, passing through undulating hills and tiny towns. The travel takes around 1.5 hours along the H5 highway.
Many highways in Italy and Slovenia use a toll system, so bring some cash with you.

Bus Connections to Trieste
If you do not want to drive, long-distance bus services are a cheap and handy alternative.
Major operators such as FlixBus and BusCenter provide trips to Trieste from destinations around Italy and Europe.

Popular routes include a 2.5-3 hour bus ride from Venice to Trieste, with frequent daily departures.
Buses from Ljubljana to Trieste run frequently, taking around 2 hours.
The bus travel from Zagreb to Trieste takes around 3-4 hours.

Ferry And Sea Routes

Trieste's prominent position on the Adriatic Sea makes coming by boat a gorgeous choice for visitors going along the coast or from adjacent cities.

The Trieste boat Terminal is located near the city center and serves a range of boat routes.

Ferry Service to Trieste
During the summer, a boat service connects Venice and Trieste. This gorgeous route follows the Adriatic shoreline and is a nice way to get between the two cities.

Ferries from Rovinj and Pula in Croatia link to Trieste, with travel times varying from 2 to 4 hours, depending on the point of departure.

Private yachts and cruise ships
Trieste is also a popular stop for yachts and cruise ships traveling along the Adriatic.
The port facilities are good, and cruise guests may simply disembark and begin seeing the city's various attractions directly from the harbor.

Border Crossing And Visa Requirements
Because of its closeness to Slovenia and Croatia, visitors from various regions of Europe frequently cross the border to Trieste.
If you are considering a multi-country journey, bear these considerations in mind:

EU and Schengen Zone Travelers
Trieste is located in Italy, which is part of the Schengen Zone.
This implies that if you are traveling from another Schengen nation (such as Slovenia or Austria), you will not have to go through border checks. You can easily cross borders with only your national ID or passport.

Non-EU Travelers
If you are traveling from outside the Schengen Zone, check sure your visa is up to date.
Many non-EU nationals need a Schengen visa to visit Italy, so verify your visa status before you go.

If you want to go to Slovenia or Croatia, be sure your visa also covers those countries.

Border crossings by car
If you are driving into Trieste from Slovenia or Croatia, prepare for passport checks at the border.

While inspections are normally brief, it is a good idea to have your passport and car registration accessible.

Whether arriving by airline, rail, automobile, or ferry, Trieste is well-connected and easily accessible. Its location at the crossroads of Italy, Slovenia, and the Adriatic makes it an attractive destination for visitors from all around.

CHAPTER 2

Best Time to Visit and Length of Stay

One of the most enjoyable aspects about visiting Trieste is its variety.

Whether you are strolling through its medieval streets in the height of summer or drinking a warm cup of coffee at a beach café during the cooler months, this delightful Italian city has something for everyone.

To really enjoy Trieste's enchantment, arrange your vacation around the weather, events, and your unique travel tastes.

This chapter will go over the seasons, the best months to visit, how long you should stay, and some of the city's major festivals and special events to consider.

Seasons Of Trieste: Weather And Events

Trieste's peculiar topography, wedged between the Adriatic Sea and the Carso Plateau foothills, results in a climate that is both Mediterranean and continental.

While the weather is quite pleasant in comparison to much of Europe, the experience in Trieste varies dramatically depending on the season.

Spring (March – May)
Spring is a wonderful time to explore Trieste.
As the city emerges from winter, the weather warms up, with temperatures ranging from 10°C to 20°C (50°F to 68°F).

The trees begin to flower, and the city's parks, such as Giardino Pubblico Muzio de Tommasini, come alive. Spring marks the beginning of the tourist season, although it is still quieter than the summer months, making it a good time for people who prefer less crowds.

In May, the city hosts Barcolana Primavera, a spring festival centered on cuisine, wine, and culture. It is a lesser version of the famed Barcolana Regatta, which takes place in the fall, but it is still worthwhile to attend.

Summer (June-August)
Summer is peak season in Trieste, with mild weather attracting people to the city's beaches and outdoor areas.
From June to August, average daily temperatures range between 20°C and 30°C (68°F to 86°F), with the warmest days in July and August.

The sea is warm enough for swimming, and the beaches of Barcola and Grado become popular with both locals and visitors.
During the summer, there are several outdoor events.

The Trieste Summer Festival offers live music, open-air movies, and street entertainment to the city's squares, while the Film Festival of Trieste draws filmgoers from all over the world.

Autumn (September–November)
Autumn is another lovely time to visit Trieste, particularly for people who like cooler temperatures.
September remains warm, with temperatures in the mid-20s °C (70s °F), but by November, temperatures have dropped to roughly 10°C to 15°C (50°F to 59°F).

One of the highlights of fall is the Barcolana Regatta, which takes place in October. This world-renowned sailing event attracts competitors from all over the world, with thousands of sailboats racing in the seas of the Gulf of Trieste.

The fall months also provide breathtaking sight as the leaves change color on the trees that line the city's slopes. The Carso Plateau is exceptionally beautiful at this time of year, with excellent hiking options among the bright fall colors.

Winter (December - February).
Trieste has comparatively moderate winters compared to other European towns, with temperatures ranging from 5°C to 10°C (41°F to 50°F).
While there may be some frigid days, snow rarely falls in the city.
Winter is the off-season for tourist, so expect fewer crowds, cheaper lodgings, and a more relaxed attitude.

December is a joyous month, with the city adorned by Christmas lights and decorations.
The center plaza of Trieste, Piazza Unità d'Italia, is home to a delightful Christmas market where you can find unique gifts and sample seasonal delights.

The Epiphany Regatta, held in early January, is a notable event during the winter season.
While smaller than the Barcolana, it is a popular race among residents and sailors.

Best Months To Travel

While Trieste is open year-round, certain months provide superior experiences depending on what you are looking for in a trip.
Here are the ideal months to travel based on your interests:

For sight-seeing and comfortable weather: April, May, September and October
If you want to see the city's historic landmarks, museums, and outdoor attractions, the spring and fall seasons are best.
The weather is good but not scorching, and the city is less busy than it is in the summer.
You will also be able to attend a variety of cultural events throughout these months.

For beach lovers: June, July, and August.
If you want to spend time by the sea, Trieste is best visited during the summer months.
You will have lots of sunny days to swim, sunbathe, and explore the Adriatic.
The ocean is warm and appealing, and there are several beach bars and restaurants operating at this time.

For budget travelers seeking a quiet experience: November to March.
Winter is the off-season in Trieste, so you will discover lower prices and less tourists.
If you prefer a more tranquil experience or to take advantage of lower prices, now is an excellent time to visit.

However, be prepared for lower temperatures and occasional rain.

For festival enthusiasts: October (Barcolana Regatta), December (Christmas Markets)
October is the finest month to attend Trieste's most famous event, the Barcolana Regatta.
Even if you do not enjoy sailing, the colorful atmosphere and varied activities are worth seeing.
December is also ideal for getting into the holiday spirit and visiting the Christmas markets.

The Ideal Length Of Stay

The length of your stay in Trieste is determined by what you hope to experience.
While the city may be visited in a few days, a longer stay allows you to discover more of its hidden beauties and take day excursions to adjacent attractions.

2-3 Days: A Brief Overview
If you do not have much time, two to three days in Trieste will be enough to explore the key sites.
You may spend a day exploring the city center, including Piazza Unità d'Italia, the Roman Theatre, and Castello di Miramare.

On the second day, visit Grotta Gigante or take a walk along the Rive shoreline.
If you have a third day, try a quick excursion to Muggia or Duino.

4-5 days for a more in-depth experience.
With four to five days, you will have more time to explore Trieste's surrounds.
In addition to the city's attractions, you may take a day excursion to Slovenia or Croatia, both of which are only a short drive away.
You will also get opportunity to explore the Carso Plateau and go hiking or wine tasting.

A week or more of full immersion.
If you intend on staying for a week or longer, you may thoroughly immerse yourself in Trieste's culture.
You will have time to see lesser-known sights, attend local festivals, and discover adjacent regions such as Friuli Venezia Giulia.

This also allows you to relax, eat the local food, and fully immerse yourself in the city's atmosphere.

Festivals And Special Events To Plan For

Throughout the year, Trieste hosts a variety of interesting festivals and events that might add to the thrill of your vacation.
If you want to plan your vacation around one of these events,
here are some of the better ones to keep in mind:

Barcolana Regatta (October)
The Barcolana Regatta is one of the world's largest and best-known sailing competitions.
This annual event, held in October, attracts hundreds of sailboats to the seas of the Gulf of Trieste.

Even if you do not participate, the event creates a festival-like atmosphere across the city, with bands, food booths, and festivities taking place all around.

Trieste Summer Festival (June-August)
Throughout the summer, the Trieste Summer Festival delivers live entertainment, music, and drama to the city's public squares.
Open-air concerts are a highlight, with both local and worldwide performers performing on stage.

It is a terrific opportunity to see Trieste's culture while basking in the balmy summer nights.

Trieste Film Festival (January).
Film enthusiasts should plan their visit for January, when the Trieste Film Festival takes place.
This international festival honours cinema, notably films from Eastern and Central Europe. Screenings, seminars, and conversations are presented in various locations across the city.

Christmas markets (December).
Trieste transforms into a winter paradise in December, complete with lovely Christmas Markets.
These markets, held at Piazza Sant'Antonio Nuovo and around the city center, provide festive decorations, handcrafted items, and a variety of local foods.

It is the ideal time to pick up holiday gifts while sipping a warm cup of vin brulé (mulled wine).

The Feria de Málaga is a well-known event in southern Spain, held annually in August.

It is a week-long celebration of flamenco music, dance, traditional costumes, food booths, and carnival attractions. Málaga's streets are bustling with activity, making it an ideal time to come if you want to experience local culture.

Noche de San Juan (June 23) is a midsummer event in which residents congregate on beaches to ignite bonfires and commemorate the longest day of the year.

Many villages around the Costa del Sol organize festivals, and it is a terrific chance to participate in the fun with the people.

Carnival (February/March) is held in many communities along the Costa del Sol, with Málaga holding the major activities.

Whether you are visiting for a weekend or a longer stay, organizing your vacation to Trieste around the correct season, event, or festival may make all the difference.

The city has much to offer all year, and by taking into account the weather, the sort of experience you seek, and the length of your visit, you can ensure that your time in Trieste is memorable.

Final Thought: The Art of Arrival

Arriving in Trieste feels like stepping into a forgotten jewel where the Adriatic whispers against neoclassical shores and faded grandeur lingers in every sunlit piazza.

From your first glimpse of its literary cafés to the meeting of sea and karst hills, you sense this isn't just a city—it's the beginning of a story only you can write.

CHAPTER 3

Top Ten Tourist Attractions in Trieste

Trieste is a city that seamlessly blends history and contemporary, with breathtaking architecture, a dynamic culture, and picturesque coastline vistas.

From majestic squares to hidden jewels, the city has attractions to suit a wide range of interests.

In this chapter, we will look at the top 10 tourist sites in Trieste, offering insightful insights and practical advice for making the most of your stay.

Piazza Unità D'Italia
Overview
Piazza Unità d'Italia, often known as the Unity of Italy Square, is Trieste's heart and soul.

It is one of Europe's largest beachfront squares, covering around 12,000 square meters.

Surrounded by gorgeous neoclassical buildings, the area is a popular gathering place for both inhabitants and tourists, symbolizing the city's rich history and dynamic culture.

Highlights
The area is home to numerous spectacular structures, including the Town Hall (Palazzo del Municipio), the Palazzo della Giunta Regionale, and the Caffe degli Specchi, a medieval café famed for its elegant decor and delicious pastries.
A dramatic fountain in the center enhances the charm of this open area.

Practical Tips
Piazza Unità d'Italia is open 24/7, making it suitable for both daytime and evening strolls.

The square is less busy in the early morning or late afternoon, making it ideal for photography.
Nearby attractions include the Grand Canal and Castello di San Giusto.

Miramare Castle Overview
Miramare fortress, also known as Castello di Miramare, is a beautiful nineteenth-century fortress located on cliffs overlooking the Adriatic Sea.
Archduke Ferdinand Maximilian of Austria commissioned it for his loving wife, and it has both Romantic and medieval architectural elements.
The castle is surrounded by a beautiful park with lush flowers and stunning sea views.

Highlights
Inside the castle, visitors may explore a number of elegantly decorated rooms, including the great hall, dining room, and private apartments, each of which provides a peek into the lives of the Austrian aristocracy.

Exotic flora, sculptures, and meandering walkways adorn the expansive gardens, making them ideal for a leisurely stroll.

Practical Tips
The castle is open from 9 AM to 7 PM during the summer, with lower hours in the winter. Always check the official website for updates.

A ticket provides admission to the castle interiors and surrounding grounds. Discounts are frequently provided for students and elders.

Getting there: Miramare Castle is a 10-minute drive from the city center, with public transit choices include buses and trams.

Overview Of The Roman Theatre

The Roman Theatre of Trieste is a historic ruin dating back to the first century AD. Located on the slopes of San Giusto Hill, this well-preserved theatre historically held around 6,000 spectators and was an important part of the city's cultural life under the Roman Empire.

Highlights
Visitors may examine the theatre's vestiges, which include a semi-circular seating area and stage.
The position also provides a great view over the city and the Gulf of Trieste.

The adjoining archeological museum gives historical information as well as other Roman artifacts.

Practical Tips
The theatre is open to the public and entry is free.
It is a popular destination, so go early in the day.

Consider taking a guided tour to gain a deeper knowledge of the site's history and significance.

Bring appropriate shoes since there are several steep paths around the theatre.

Grand Canal (Canal Grande)

Overview
The Grand Canal, also known as Canal Grande, is a magnificent canal that serves as a reminder of Trieste's nautical legacy.

It is a dynamic district filled with colorful buildings, cafés, and stores that encapsulate the essence of the city's multiculturalism.

Highlights
Strolling down the canal, you will see beautiful bridges, bustling markets, and the lovely Church of San Antonio Nuovo, which is noted for its distinctive architecture.

The area becomes especially bustling in the evening, when locals and visitors congregate to enjoy the atmosphere and dine al fresco.

Practical Tips
Dining options include restaurants and cafés along the canal serving fresh fish and local cuisine. Trattoria Da Giovanni serves traditional Triestine meals.

The best time to visit is early evening, when the sun sets over the canal, providing a lovely vista.
Take a boat cruise to experience Trieste's architecture from a different viewpoint.

Revoltella Museum Overview

The Revoltella Museum is a contemporary art museum focused to the nineteenth and twentieth centuries, located in a stunning modern structure.

It was founded on the bequest of Baron Revoltella, a prominent player in Trieste's cultural scene who left his collection to the city.

Highlights:
The museum exhibits modern and contemporary art from both local and foreign artists.
The wonderfully constructed interior is as remarkable as the artwork on show, and the museum frequently holds temporary exhibits, seminars, and cultural events.

Practical Tips
The museum is open from 10 AM to 7 PM (closed on Mondays). Always double-check the hours because they might change.
Admission rates are reasonable, including reductions for students and elderly.

Group pricing are also available for educational institutions.
The museum is conveniently placed within walking distance of the city center, making it an ideal complement to any itinerary.

Overview Of The Cathedral Of San Giusto

The Cathedral of San Giusto, also known as Cattedrale di San Giusto, is Trieste's principal church and is noteworthy in both history and religion.

It is located on Trieste's highest point and provides breathtaking views of the city and its surroundings.

Highlights
The cathedral combines architectural styles, including Romanesque and Gothic components.

Inside, you will see exquisite mosaics, altars, and a gorgeous apse filled with vibrant artwork. The surrounding San Giusto Castle, with its fortress-like construction and panoramic vistas, adds another level of interest to the visit.

Practical Tips
Visiting Hours: The cathedral is normally open from 7 AM to 7 PM, with mass services on Sundays.
Check for religious events that may impact visitor access.

Dress Code: Modest clothes is encouraged at religious locations.
Cover your shoulders and knees before entering.
After touring the cathedral, explore the nearby castle and park for a full experience.

San Sabba Rice Mill Overview
The San Sabba Rice Mill, also known as Ex Stabilimento Riso, is a former rice mill that has been converted into a museum, providing a gloomy but vital glimpse into Trieste's history during WWII.
It was originally a concentration camp and is now a monument and educational facility.

Highlights:
Visitors may explore the former mill and learn about the history of rice farming, including darker parts.
The exhibits contain images, papers, and human accounts that give a vivid picture of the lives affected by the events that occurred here.

Practical Tips
Admission is often free, however contributions are appreciated to fund upkeep and educational activities.
Consider taking a guided tour to learn more about the site's history and significance.

Audio tutorials are also available in several languages.
The site's sensitive history encourages visitors to approach exhibits with respect and consideration.

Museo Di Storia Naturale Overview

The Natural History Museum in Trieste is a great place for families and nature enthusiasts.
The museum, housed in a beautifully renovated structure, has a large collection of natural history artifacts, ranging from fossils to stuffed animals.

Highlights
The exhibitions cover a variety of themes, including geology, paleontology, and biodiversity.
Highlights include dinosaur bones, mineral collections, and interactive exhibits that make learning enjoyable for people of all ages.

Practical Tips
The museum is typically open from 9 AM to 7 PM, with additional hours for weekends and holidays.

Family-Friendly Activities: Look for seminars and educational events, especially during school vacations, making it an ideal destination for families.
After your visit, take a walk around surrounding parks including Giardino Pubblico Muzio de Tommasini to relax and enjoy nature.

Overview Of The Historical Museum In Trieste

The Museo Storico di Trieste provides an in-depth study at the city's history, from its origins as a Roman town to its role as an important port in the Austro-Hungarian Empire.
Housed in a majestic edifice, the museum offers an intriguing voyage through time.

Highlights
The displays contain relics, artworks, and papers depicting Trieste's rich past.
Notable exhibits highlight nautical history and the city's importance as a major Adriatic port.
The museum regularly presents temporary exhibits that offer new insights on certain historical topics.

Practical Tips
Admission fees: The entrance prices are low, with reductions available for students and elderly.
Group trips can be organized for educational objectives.
Aim for a mid-week visit to avoid crowds and have a more personalized experience with the displays.
Book a guided tour to fully comprehend Trieste's fascinating history.

The Lighthouse Of Trieste
Overview
The Trieste Lighthouse, also known as the Faro della Vittoria, is a landmark that stands 70 meters (230 ft) tall.
Built in the early twentieth century, it is both an operating lighthouse and a symbol of the city.

Highlights:
Visitors may climb the lighthouse to enjoy panoramic views of Trieste, the surrounding shoreline, and the Adriatic Sea.
The surrounding neighborhood has wonderful promenades that are ideal for a leisurely walk.

Practical Tips
Opening Hours: The lighthouse is often open throughout summer months, however check local listings for exact visit times.
Bring comfortable shoes for the hike, which entails several stairs.
Do not forget your camera for the breathtaking sights!

The best time to visit is in the late afternoon for a stunning sunset vista over the Adriatic.

Overview of San Giusto Castle and Cathedral (4.6)

San Giusto Castle (Castello di San Giusto), perched atop San Giusto Hill, is an outstanding 15th-century castle.

It provides panoramic views of the city and the Adriatic Sea, making it a must-see for anybody visiting Trieste.
The castle's construction recalls the region's military importance under the Austro-Hungarian Empire.

Highlights of the castle include well-preserved ramparts, turrets, and a modest museum showcasing Trieste's military past.

The Cathedral of San Giusto, located close to the castle, is a must-see.
This cathedral boasts stunning mosaics, altars, and an intriguing mix of architectural styles, principally Romanesque and Gothic.

The Cathedral of San Giusto
This cathedral, dedicated to Trieste's patron saint, is notable for its stunning interior and rich history. It holds numerous significant items of art, including a magnificent altar and reliquaries.

Practical Tips
The castle is open from 9 AM to 7 PM during summer and reduced hours in winter.
The cathedral keeps similar hours.

Admission Fees: The castle grounds need a nominal charge, while the cathedral is free to see.
The best time to visit is in the early morning to avoid crowds and enjoy the sights peacefully.

Getting There: A short trek from the city center leads to the castle, with gorgeous roads and gardens along the way.

Synagogue Of Trieste Overview

The Synagogue of Trieste, or Tempio Israelitico, is one of Europe's biggest synagogues, constructed in 1912.
It is an outstanding example of Moorish Revival architecture, distinguished by its beautiful domes and detailed ornamentation.

The Jewish community in Trieste has a long history extending back to the Roman Empire, making this location especially noteworthy. The synagogue's interior showcases the Jewish community's religious and cultural legacy, with stunning stained glass and intricate ornamentation.

Visitors may learn about the history of Jews in Trieste and how they contributed to the city's development.

Practical Tips
Visiting Hours: The synagogue is usually open on weekdays, but check for exact hours and schedule a guided tour.
Visitors must dress modestly since this is a place of worship. Make careful to cover your shoulders and knees.

Guided tours offer insights into the synagogue's history and architecture, enriching the experience.
The synagogue is easily accessible by foot from Piazza Unità d'Italia, making it a convenient addition to any itinerary.

Overview Of Trieste's Old Port (Porto Vecchio)

Porto Vecchio is Trieste's historic port sector, a picturesque location that represents the city's nautical tradition.

The port, which was once a thriving powerhouse of trade and commerce, has seen a number of changes over time.

Today, it stands as a reminder of the city's industrial heritage, with exquisite architecture and breathtaking waterfront vistas.

Highlights

The region has remarkable old warehouses and industries, many of which are being renovated for modern usage.

Walking around the shoreline, you may see the relics of former piers and shipyards.

The neighboring Molo Audace has a nice promenade perfect for strolling, with views of the Adriatic Sea and the surrounding hills.

Practical Tips

The best time to visit is late afternoon for stunning sunset views across the bay, particularly from Molo Audace.

Photography: The contrast of ancient industrial structures against the backdrop of the sea creates fascinating photos.

Events: This neighborhood hosts cultural events, festivals, and markets, creating a bustling ambiance for visitors.

Porto Vecchio is easily accessible by foot from the city center, making it an ideal stop for your journey.

Val Rosandra Natural Reserve

Overview
Val Rosandra is a magnificent natural reserve just outside Trieste known for its gorgeous views and diverse wildlife.
The reserve is marked by sheer cliffs, thick trees, and a flowing river, making it an ideal destination for nature lovers and hikers.

Highlights
The reserve has various hiking paths, ranging from easy treks to more difficult climbs that go up to the cliffs for great views of the surrounding region.

Wildlife is rich here, with several bird species and a distinct vegetation. The neighboring Rosandra River adds to the visual charm and allows for swimming during the warmer months.

Practical Tips
The best time to visit: Spring and early fall are good for trekking due to nice weather and colorful vegetation.
Maps are provided at the reserve's entry, and defined paths make navigation easy.

What to pack: Wear strong hiking shoes and pack plenty of water, especially if you intend to hike during the warmer months.

Getting there: The reserve is accessible by public transit, with various bus lines linking it to the city center. Alternatively, consider driving for greater convenience.

Vittoria Light (Faro della Vittoria)
Overview
The Vittoria Light, also known as Faro della Vittoria, is a well-known lighthouse situated on the cliffs of the Borgo Teresiano area. Completed in 1927, it is 70 meters (230 feet) tall and is a major landmark in Trieste.

The lighthouse was erected to remember the fallen troops of World War I and to commemorate the city's maritime history.

Highlights
Visitors may climb to the top of the lighthouse to enjoy beautiful views over Trieste and the Adriatic Sea.

The ascent is a succession of stairs, but the reward at the summit is worthwhile.

On a clear day, you can view well beyond the city, including the shoreline and surrounding islands.

Practical Tips
Check local listings for particular hours of operation for the lighthouse, which is normally open during summer months. Bring comfortable footwear and a camera to capture spectacular sights throughout the climb.

The best time to visit is late afternoon or sunset for optimal photo opportunities and a wonderful experience as the sun sets below the horizon.

The lighthouse is easily accessible from the city center and has close parking.
It is also accessible by public transportation, followed by a short walk.

Trieste is a city with a diverse range of attractions, all steeped in history and natural beauty.
From the historic walls of San Giusto Castle to the bustling atmosphere of Porto Vecchio, these locations illustrate the city's multifaceted personality.

Whether you are touring old churches, hiking in tranquil nature reserves, or admiring architectural marvels, Trieste offers an exceptional experience for every visitor.

Each attraction allows you to explore further into this coastal gem's unique narrative, ensuring that your stay is both fun and enriching.

CHAPTER 4

Where to Stay: Accommodation in Trieste

Finding the ideal hotel to stay in Trieste may greatly improve your vacation experience.

Trieste, with its rich history, gorgeous architecture, and active culture, has a diverse selection of lodging alternatives to meet the demands and budgets of all travelers.

Whether you want luxury, affordability, or a one-of-a-kind boutique experience, this chapter will walk you through the many options accessible in this fascinating city.

Overview Of Accommodation Options

Trieste offers a wide range of lodging alternatives, from high-end luxury hotels to lovely budget hostels.

Each neighborhood in the city has its own distinct character, so where you stay might impact your whole experience.

Luxurious Resorts: Trieste's premium hotels provide top-notch facilities, beautiful vistas, and great service for visitors looking to indulge.
These businesses frequently have on-site restaurants, spas, and fitness centers, offering a relaxed and luxurious visit.

Budget-Friendly Hotels: Travelers may choose affordable hotels and hostels that provide excellent accommodations without breaking the bank.
Many of these alternatives provide clean, modest lodging with convenient access to public transit and local attractions.

For a personalized experience, boutique guesthouses and bed-and-breakfasts are excellent options.

These smaller enterprises frequently represent the local culture and friendliness, offering distinctive design, home-cooked cuisine, and a cozy ambiance.

Holiday Rentals: Trieste offers a choice of holiday rentals, including flats and houses.
These might be an excellent alternative for families or parties traveling together, as they provide additional room and the opportunity to prepare their meals.

For lone travelers or those wishing to meet new people, Trieste's hostels provide reasonable accomodation and public places for mingling.

Many hostels arrange activities and trips to assist visitors experience the city.

Luxury Resorts

Trieste has numerous luxury resorts that guarantee sumptuous accommodations. Here are some top picks:

Hotel Savoia Excelsior Palace.

Hotel Savoia Excelsior Palace, located on the waterfront, offers both historical elegance and modern comforts.
The hotel offers attractively designed rooms with breathtaking views of the Gulf of Trieste.

Amenities include a full-service spa, workout center, and rooftop terrace with stunning sunset views.

The on-site restaurant specializes on superb Italian food made using locally sourced ingredients.

Ideal for couples seeking a romantic retreat or those who value elegance and comfort.

Hilton Garden Inn Trieste

The hotel has a modern style and ideal position in the heart of Trieste.
The Hilton Garden Inn is suitable for both business and leisure travellers.

Amenities include large rooms, rooftop patio, and fitness center.
The restaurant serves a variety of Italian and foreign meals.
Ideal for business travelers and families seeking comfort and convenience.

Grand Hotel Duchi d'Aosta

Located on Piazza Unità d'Italia, this historic hotel offers elegance and a prime position.
It provides amazing views of the square and the sea.

The hotel has a gourmet restaurant, spa facility, and tastefully decorated rooms. Guests may unwind in the hotel's comfortable lounges or on the patio.

Perfect for those seeking traditional luxury and a central location.

Hotel Continentale

The hotel's contemporary style and strategic location provide guests quick access to Trieste's attractions.

Amenities include spacious rooms, a bar, and a health center with sauna and workout equipment. Breakfast is provided in a sophisticated dining room and includes a variety of local specialties.

Ideal for travelers looking for a contemporary style and exceptional service.

Budget-Friendly Hotels

Trieste has several affordable choices that offer great value without sacrificing comfort.
Here are a few prominent hotels:

Hotel Italia

Located in the city center, this family-run hotel offers warm welcome and a friendly ambiance.

The hotel provides simple yet pleasant rooms with contemporary conveniences.

A complementary breakfast is provided, which includes fresh pastries and coffee.
Perfect for budget tourists seeking a welcoming atmosphere and customized service.

Hotel Central
Conveniently positioned among key sites, Hotel Central serves as an ideal base for exploring.
Free Wi-Fi and breakfast are available in the modest yet comfortable lodgings.
The personnel is noted for their helpfulness and local knowledge.
Ideal for backpackers and lone travelers seeking cost and ease.

B&B Hotel Trieste
Overview: This contemporary hotel is part of the B&B group and provides great accommodation at affordable costs.
Amenities include free Wi-Fi, a buffet breakfast, and comfortable rooms with basic amenities.
The location is great for those looking to see the city's attractions.
Ideal for families and groups looking for affordable, roomy lodgings.

Hostel Della Gioventù
This hostel is ideal for young tourists and backpackers due to its affordable price and convenient location.

Amenities include dormitory and private rooms, a community kitchen, and social areas.

Guests can participate in organized excursions and activities. Perfect for solo travelers wishing to meet new people and save money on accommodations.

Boutique Guesthouses
Trieste's boutique guesthouses are ideal for guests looking for a one-of-a-kind and personalized experience.
Here are a few things to consider:

Casa de Maria
is a delightful hostel housed in a historic structure with tastefully designed rooms reflecting local culture.

Amenities include a lounge, garden, and complementary breakfast with local food.
The hosts are well-known for their kind service and knowledge of the area.

Ideal for couples or people seeking a personalized, cozy setting.

B&B Il Volo
Overview: B&B Il Volo prioritizes comfort and service for a memorable stay.
The guesthouse's central location allows you to easily explore Trieste.

Amenities: Tastefully designed rooms with private bathrooms. Guests may enjoy a handmade breakfast with fresh, local food.

Ideal for travelers who value individual attention and a welcoming setting.

La Casa di Otto
Overview: This boutique guesthouse offers a unique experience by combining modern amenities and historical charm.

Amenities include individually decorated rooms, a pleasant common area, and a gorgeous patio.

Breakfast is offered everyday, and the staff may provide local recommendations.

Ideal for those seeking a memorable stay in a unique location.

Afittacamere Aunus
Affittacamere Aunus, housed in a historic property, provides elegant rooms with a warm ambiance.

Amenities include continental breakfast, free Wi-Fi, and a communal kitchen.
The guesthouse is renowned for its cleanliness and attention to detail.

Perfect for budget-conscious travelers seeking a boutique experience.

Unique Stays

When visiting Trieste, consider staying somewhere one-of-a-kind that provides a unique experience. Here are some possibilities that provide character, charm, and a feeling of place:

A Boutique Hotel inside a Historic Villa

Overview: Staying in a historic villa provides a unique insight into Trieste's architectural legacy.
Many of these homes have been refurbished and converted into boutique hotels that blend elegance with modern comforts.

Experience: Guests may enjoy elegantly decorated rooms, lush gardens, and wonderful views of the surrounding countryside.
These villas frequently have rich histories and distinct tales, which give richness to your visit.
Recommend Villa Braida or Villa Neri as a calm hideaway near the city core.

A Floating Hotel
Overview: Staying aboard a floating hotel offers a unique and unforgettable experience.
This option is offered at numerous marinas in Trieste, offering a unique view of the city from the sea.

Experience: Imagine waking up to the peaceful sound of waves and a glimpse of the harbor.
Floating hotels frequently provide contemporary facilities such as comfy mattresses, baths, and tiny kitchens.

Consider staying at the Marina di Trieste, where you may reserve a cabin on a houseboat or yacht for a unique experience.

Turned Industrial Spaces: Trieste's former factories and warehouses have been cleverly turned into stylish lodgings, reflecting the city's rich industrial history.

These areas typically have high ceilings, exposed brick, and industrial design, creating a sleek and contemporary environment.

Staying in these locations allows you to experience Trieste's heritage while enjoying modern amenities.

Recommendation: The Tergesteo Hotel has a prime position and combines modern and historical design aspects.

Agriturismo Retreats. Agriturismos provide a peaceful hideaway in the countryside for those seeking a break from city life.

These farm-stays provide an opportunity to experience rural living while also enjoying locally produced cuisine and wine.

Experience the splendor of the surrounding countryside, participate in farm activities, and eat great prepared meals.

Many agriturismi are located within a short drive from Trieste, making them ideal for day getaways.

Recommendation: Agriturismo San Vito, located in the hills, offers breathtaking vistas and traditional gastronomic experiences.

Top Recommended Accommodations

While Trieste's hotel scene is broad, many places routinely earn excellent marks for their service, comfort, and distinctive offers.
Here are some highly recommended places:

Hotel Regent
Located on the Gulf of Trieste, Hotel Regent offers exquisite rooms with beautiful views.

The hotel has large rooms with modern design, a wellness center, and an outdoor pool.

Guests may also enjoy a gourmet restaurant that focuses on local food. Ideal for travelers looking for a relaxing and elegant experience.

Hotel Tergesteo
Located in a historic building, Hotel Tergesteo offers a beautiful and comfortable stay in the city centre.

The hotel has contemporary design and modern facilities, including an on-site bar, fitness facility, and complementary breakfast.

It is a wonderful pick for individuals who value both style and comfort. Ideal for trend-conscious travelers seeking a central location.

B&B Sogni D'Oro.

Overview: A beautiful bed-and-breakfast that embodies Trieste's warmth. The welcoming environment and customized treatment make it a popular destination for travelers.

Amenities include pleasant rooms with en-suite bathrooms and a handmade breakfast with local ingredients.
Ideal for travelers seeking a personalized, home-like experience.

Hotel Colle Di Ronda

Overview: This hotel on the outskirts of Trieste provides a calm respite with spectacular views of the city and sea.

Amenities include large rooms, a garden, and outdoor lounging places. In addition, the hotel's restaurant provides traditional local food.

Ideal for nature enthusiasts and those wanting a peaceful hideaway near to the city.

Selecting The Suitable Accommodation For You

When choosing the best Trieste lodging, numerous elements must be considered to ensure a pleasant and happy stay.
Here are some guidelines to help you make your decision:

Determine your budget before beginning your search.
Trieste has a variety of possibilities, so knowing how much you are ready to pay can help you limit down your selections.
Remember to factor in other expenditures, including as taxes and prospective fees for services like parking or breakfast.

Decide on your visit location and activities.
If you intend to see historical landmarks, lodging in the city center may be excellent.
If you want a quieter ambiance, try staying a little away of the main tourist regions. Access to public transit can also make a big difference.

Type of Experience.
Decide what type of experience you desire.
Are you seeking for luxury and indulgence, or do you prefer a comfortable guesthouse?
Unique accommodations such as agriturismi or floating hotels can give remarkable experiences that improve your trip.

Amenities and Service.
Consider the facilities that are vital to you.
Free Wi-Fi, breakfast options, and on-site parking may all enhance your visit. If you intend to cook, seek for lodgings that include a kitchen. Check the reviews to discover what other visitors have said about the quality of services and amenities.

Review and Recommendations.
Conduct some research by reading reviews on travel websites and forums.
Guest reviews might give information on the quality of the lodgings and the level of service to expect.
Friends and travel bloggers might also recommend hidden gems.

Booking Tips And Tricks

Finding the ideal hotel to stay in Trieste is critical for a positive trip experience.

Here are some suggestions to help you choose the best hotel for your needs:

Book in advance.
Trieste may grow crowded, particularly during high tourist seasons and events.
Booking your hotel in advance guarantees that you have the finest selections and might help you get a better deal.

Use Comparison Sites.
Use internet travel agents and comparison websites to compare rates and features.
Websites such as Booking.com, Expedia, and Airbnb allow you to filter results depending on your tastes, making it easy to select the ideal location.

Check for special offers.
Many hotels and guesthouses provide special bargains or packages, particularly during the off-peak season.
Look for specials that offer free nights, food savings, or complementary activities to help you enjoy your visit.

Contact Properties Directly.
Consider calling out immediately once you have found a home you like.
Some hotels provide higher prices or unique discounts for bookings made through their own websites or over the phone.
This also gives you the opportunity to ask any questions you have regarding the property.

Consider Cancellation Policies.
Before confirming your reservation, examine the cancelation rules. Flexible cancellation options might give you piece of mind if your plans alter suddenly.

Loyalty Programs
If you often stay at the same hotel chain, consider joining their reward program.
Members frequently receive incentives such as lower prices, hotel upgrades, and other amenities that improve their travel experience.

Read the fine print
Before finalizing your reservation, carefully review the costs, facilities, and check-in/check-out timings.
Being informed helps you avoid surprises upon arrival.

Understanding the many lodging alternatives available in Trieste allows you to pick the ideal place to stay that meets your needs and budget.

Whether you select a luxurious resort, a one-of-a-kind floating hotel, or a modest guesthouse, Trieste guarantees a pleasant atmosphere that will improve your trip experience.

With careful planning and thought, your visit to this enchanting city will be unforgettable, letting you to thoroughly immerse yourself in its rich history and lively culture.

CHAPTER 5

Trieste for Foodies—Where and What to Eat

Trieste, a city where cultures collide, has a thriving culinary sector that reflects its rich history and numerous influences.

Foodies will discover a plethora of excellent alternatives to explore, including traditional meals steeped in local customs, contemporary cafés, and busy markets.

This chapter will take you through the must-try meals, the best restaurants, and the city's growing coffee and wine culture.

Traditional Triestine Dishes

Trieste's food is a fascinating combination of Italian, Austrian, and Slavic influences. Here are some typical delicacies that you can not miss:

Jota
Jota, a substantial soup prepared with fermented cabbage, beans, potatoes, and sometimes smoked pig, exemplifies Triestine comfort cuisine.

Each family has their own variety, resulting in a meal rich in local customs. It is especially popular during the winter months.

Sarde at Saor
Sardines are marinated in a sweet-and-sour sauce prepared with onions, vinegar, and raisins.
The taste combination represents Trieste's marine roots, and it is a favorite antipasto in local eateries.

Strucolo di Patate
Strucolo de Patate, a savory potato and cheese-filled pasta, is similar to gnocchi but has a unique texture.
It is a soothing dish that works well in any season, especially when served with butter and sage or a rich meat sauce.

Cacciucco
Cacciucco, a classic fish stew, contains a variety of shellfish, tomatoes, and fragrant herbs.
It is robust and savory, and is frequently served with toasted bread.

Fritole
These delicious, deep-fried pastries are quite popular during Carnival season.
They are made with flour, eggs, and raisins and are frequently coated with powdered sugar before being served warm.

Kraški Pršut
This dry-cured ham from the Karst area near Trieste is recognized for its strong taste.
It is often served thinly sliced as an antipasto, accompanied by local cheeses and olives.

Torta di Prugne
The plum cake is a popular treat in Trieste.
It is cooked with fresh plums, sugar, and a buttery crust and is typically served with a cup of coffee or tea.

Best Local Restaurants
When it comes to dining, Trieste has a variety of restaurants delivering traditional and trendy food.
Here are a few top recommendations:

Trattoria da Giovanni
This trattoria is a local favorite, serving traditional Triestine meals in a friendly setting.
Saor is well-known for its Jota and Sarde, making it an ideal place to sample traditional tastes.

Osteria di Marino
Osteria da Marino, located along the Grand Canal, is well-known for its seafood specialties.
The Cacciucco is a highlight here, and its warm, friendly atmosphere makes it a must-see.

Restaurante Al Bagatto
Al Bagatto's cuisine mixes classic Triestine dishes with modern flair, providing an interesting eating experience.
The exquisite environment is ideal for a special event, and the staff is renowned for their expert wine pairings.

Hostia Malcanton
This rustic café, nestled away in the center of Trieste, is famed for its handmade pasta and local wines.
The Strucolo de Patate here is a local favorite, and the cozy atmosphere makes it ideal for a quiet evening.

Café degli Specchi
This old café, located on Piazza Unità d'Italia, provides spectacular views as well as a delicious food.
While it is well-known for its coffee, the pastries and light meals are also worth sampling.

Ristorante la Torre
La Torre's magnificent view of the Gulf of Trieste makes it perfect for a romantic meal.
The restaurant focuses on fresh seafood and local wines, ensuring a great dining experience.

Pizzeria da Michele
Pizzeria Da Michele is ideal for a relaxed supper.
It is a terrific place to relax after a day of visiting the city, known for its thin-crust pizzas and lively environment.

Cafés And Coffee Culture In Trieste

Trieste is well-known for its coffee culture, which stems from its historical links to the Austro-Hungarian Empire.
The city has various cafés, each with its own unique charm and history.

Here are some must-see spots:

Caffè Florian
Caffè Florian, founded in 1720, is one of the oldest cafés in Italy.
Its sumptuous rooms and outdoor chairs provide a luxury coffee experience.
Do not miss out on their outstanding espresso served with a classic pastry.

Café degli Specchi
As previously said, this café is a local favorite. The outside terrace is ideal for people-watching while sipping a thick cappuccino or eating a slice of Torta di Prugne.

Café San Marco
Caffè San Marco is a cultural hotspot for writers and artists, with a rich literary past.
The café has a friendly environment and serves a range of coffees, pastries, and light snacks.

Caffe Rossetti
This tiny cafe is ideal for a short coffee break.
It is a terrific place to unwind after a day of seeing the city, thanks to its courteous service and delicious espresso drinks.

Café Tommaseo
Another old café, Caffè Tommaseo, is well-known among residents for its laid-back environment.
It offers a wide selection of coffees, pastries, and small meals, making it suitable for breakfast or a noon snack.

Wine And Aperitivo Spots

Trieste's wine culture is as diverse as its culinary traditions, with numerous local vineyards producing high-quality wines.
The city also celebrates the Italian custom of aperitivo, making it simple to discover wonderful places to drink before dinner.

Enoteca Skerlj
This wine bar serves a well chosen range of local and Italian wines, as well as delectable small appetizers.
The expert staff can assist you select the ideal wine to complement your aperitivo.

Café Barbacan
Caffè Barbacan is a vibrant venue for after-work drinks with a wide range of wines and a friendly environment.
Outdoor seating is ideal for spending a warm evening.

Court of Moli
This wine shop and bar provides tastings and a diverse selection of local wines. It is an excellent site to learn about Trieste's winemaking and try different varietals.

Restaurant Pizzeria Riva del Mandracchio
Located near the waterfront, this restaurant features an excellent wine collection and a gorgeous outside patio for aperitivo.
The lively environment makes it a popular destination in the evening.

Vino and Vini
Vino e Vini is a quaint wine bar that focuses on local wines.
They provide tastings and small meals in a casual setting.
It is ideal for relaxing after a day of touring.

Street Food & Markets

For a more informal eating experience, Trieste features a strong street food scene and bustling markets.

Here's where you may indulge:

Piazza Di Cavana Market

This lively market has local sellers offering fresh fruit, cheeses, meats, and street cuisine.

While visiting the vendors, make sure to taste a slice of Fritole.

Market Coperto

This covered market, located in the city center, is a foodie's dream. There are local specialties, fresh fish, and handmade items available here.

It is a great place to get a quick lunch or fill up on local specialties.

Street vendors

Keep a look out for street sellers selling local favorites such as hot sandwiches, pastries, and seasonal delicacies.

A favorite alternative is the Panino con Porchetta, a delicious sandwich prepared from roasted pig.

Gelato Stands.

No trip to Trieste is complete without indulging in some gelato. Numerous gelaterias across the city deliver delectable tastes produced with high-quality ingredients.

Try a scoop of Stracciatella or Pistachio!

Local bakeries

Trieste is home to several bakeries that serve freshly baked goodies. Visit a local bakery for a quick breakfast or snack; the Cornetti (Italian croissants) and Pan di Ramerino (rosemary bread) are popular options.

Trieste is a foodie's paradise, with a culinary environment that encourages exploration and discovery.

Whether you are dining on traditional meals, sipping coffee in a historic café, or sipping a bottle of local wine, the city's culinary delights will leave you with memorable memories.

Dive into the tastes of Trieste and let your taste buds to take you on an extraordinary gastronomic adventure.

CHAPTER 6

Transportation in Trieste

Trieste's effective public transit infrastructure and compact size make it easy to get about.

Whether you prefer busses, renting a vehicle, or exploring on foot, this chapter will offer an overview of your alternatives for getting around this attractive city.

Public Transportation (Bus And Trams)

Trieste Trasporti operates a stable and well-connected public transportation system.

The network comprises buses and trams that travel around the city and adjacent areas, making it easy to move from one destination to another.

Buses
Buses are the principal means of public transit in Trieste, linking the city center to neighborhoods, suburbs, and adjacent attractions via many routes.

Buses operate regularly, especially during peak hours, making them an easy choice for both locals and visitors.
Tickets may be purchased at kiosks, buses (with a fee), or mobile applications.

To prevent penalties, always confirm your ticket before boarding. Single tickets are good for 75 minutes from the time they are validated, allowing for transfers between buses and trams.

Key roads connect major locations such as Miramare Castle, Val Rosandra Nature Reserve, and the main rail station.

Route Renting A Car Or Scooter

Renting A Car Or Scooter
Renting a vehicle or scooter is a great way to explore Trieste and its surrounds at your own leisure.
When renting a car in Trieste, there are several rental businesses available, both international and local.
Rental offices may be found at both the airport and around the city.

Driving in Trieste. The roads in and around Trieste are typically well maintained.
However, be warned that parking in the city center might be difficult, particularly during busy tourist seasons.

Paid parking is provided, and parking lots are located around the city. Renting a car allows for day outings to local sites, such as the seaside villages of Muggia and Sistiana or the scenic Karst area.

Renting a scooter
Renting a scooter might provide a more adventurous experience.
It is a popular way to get around the city, especially in the summer months.

Rental Services: Local firms provide scooter rentals.
Make sure you have a valid driver's license and review the rental company's terms and restrictions.

Scooters are easy to park and provide rapid access to the city's small alleyways and hidden beauties.

Taxi And Ride-Sharing Services
Taxis are easily accessible in Trieste, making it a convenient choice for individuals who do not want to take public transportation or drive.

Taxis are available for hailing on the street or at designated stands around the city.
Major hotels provide cab services to their visitors.

Taxi rates are metered and might vary depending on the time of day.
It is best to confirm the anticipated fee with the driver before beginning your journey.

Local Tip: Download a taxi app for easy booking, especially during peak hours or late at night.

Ridesharing Services
Uber and other rideshare services are available in Trieste, offering an alternative to traditional taxis.

Use a rideshare app to request a ride straight from your location, making it a convenient option for city travel or airport transportation.

Walking And Biking Across The City

Trieste is a tiny city that is best explored on foot or by bike.

Walking
Walking is a great way to experience the city's beautiful architecture, breathtaking views, and dynamic atmosphere.

Key sights such as Piazza Unità d'Italia, Miramare Castle, and the Grand Canal are easily accessible by foot.

Take a guided walking tour to learn about the city's history and culture.
Many local firms provide themed trips that cover anything from Trieste's coffee culture to its marine past.

Biking
Bike Rentals: Rent a bike and explore the city at your own speed. You may also discover bike-sharing programs, which allow you to pick up and drop off bikes at a variety of locations.

Bicycle trails in Trieste connect picturesque sites such as the shoreline and adjacent hills.

A favorite route is along the waterfront, which offers great views of the Gulf of Trieste.

Remember to bring a helmet and follow local cycling regulations for a safe and fun ride.

Ferry Service And Day Trips From Trieste
Trieste's position on the Adriatic Sea gives it an ideal base for visiting adjacent coastal locations by boat.

Ferry Services
Overview: Trieste's port connects to adjacent islands and coastal towns via various ferry companies.
Popular routes include those to Croatia and Slovenia, making it easier to discover new places.

Ferries may transport you to beautiful destinations such as Pula, Rovinj, and the islands of Cres and Krk.
Each area has its own set of attractions, ranging from breathtaking beaches to historical landmarks.

Tickets may be purchased online or at the ferry station. It is recommended to reserve in advance, especially during the summer months when boats can fill up rapidly.

Day trips
Exploring Istria: A boat voyage to this region offers many opportunities for exploration. Pula and Rovinj are famed for their stunning architecture, Roman ruins, and delectable food.

The Slovenian shore is easily accessible from Trieste.
Consider taking a day trip to Piran, a picturesque beach town noted for its ancient architecture and breathtaking vistas.

Local tip: Bring your camera!
The views from the ferries and seaside towns are beautiful and ideal for photographing special occasions.

Trieste's excellent public transportation system, pedestrian-friendly streets, and picturesque bicycle paths make it easy to navigate.

Whether you want to explore on foot, hire a car, or take a ferry for a day excursion, Trieste has a variety of transportation alternatives to meet any traveler's preferences.

Enjoy the adventure as you discover the beauty and charm of this magnificent city!

CHAPTER 7

Practical Tips for Your Stay

When traveling to Trieste, having a few practical advice on hand will improve your experience and guarantee a pleasant visit.

This chapter provides critical information about money, safety, communication, connection, and health services, allowing you to confidently traverse the city.

Currency And Payment

Trieste, like the rest of Italy, has the Euro as its official currency.
Understanding how to manage money throughout your stay will help you prevent unneeded stress.

Currency exchange services are provided in banks, exchange offices, and select hotels.

Airport exchange desks are handy, although they may provide less advantageous rates.

For the greatest exchange rates, try withdrawing cash from city ATMs.

ATMs are extensively available in Trieste and most accept foreign cards. You can withdraw cash in Euros, but verify your bank's foreign transaction costs.

Payments
Most restaurants, stores, and hotels in Trieste accept credit and debit cards like Visa and MasterCard.
However, some smaller venues may only accept cash, so bring some Euros for purchases at markets or tiny cafés.

Tipping: Tipping is not mandatory in Italy.
However, rounding up the amount or leaving a small tip (about 5-10%) for outstanding service is greatly appreciated.

Safety Tips And Emergency Numbers

Trieste is considered a safe city for travelers, although as with any vacation, it is prudent to remain attentive and adhere to basic safety precautions.

General Safety Tips
Be Aware: Be aware of your surroundings, particularly in congested locations and on public transit.

Keep your valuables safe, and avoid exhibiting pricey goods.

Beware of Scams: Be wary of those begging for donations or selling products aggressively.

If anything feels odd, follow your instincts and go on.

Emergency Numbers
Knowing the appropriate numbers is critical in an emergency:
Police: 112 (general emergency)
Ambulance/Fire Service: 118
Local Police Station: 113.

If you want medical attention, do not hesitate to dial these numbers or visit the local hospital.

Language: Communicating In Trieste
Trieste's official language is Italian, however due to the city's historical links to other cultures, you will hear a variety of languages.

Basic Italian phrases
While many people, particularly in the hotel business, understand English, knowing a few basic Italian words might enhance your experience:

Greetings: Ciao (casual), Buongiorno (good morning)
Thanks: Grazie.
Request: Per favore.
Excuse me. Scusi
Do you speak English (Parla inglese)?

Communication Tips:
Be patient.
If you face a linguistic problem, be patient. Most people appreciate your efforts to converse in Italian, even if it is only a few words.

Use Translation Apps: Having a translation app on your phone can assist overcome language barriers and improve communication with locals.

Wifi And Staying Connected
Staying connected while visiting Trieste is essential for navigating, communicating, and sharing your experiences.

Wi-Fi Availability
Free Wi-Fi is available at many cafés, restaurants, and public locations in Trieste.

Look for "Wi-Fi" indicators or ask staff for access.
Libraries, shopping malls, and parks are among the most popular destinations.

Trieste's municipal Wi-Fi network, "Wi-Fi Trieste," offers free internet access in public spaces.
You may need to sign up for access.

Mobile connectivity
Consider acquiring a local SIM card for frequent phone use.
Several carriers provide prepaid choices with data plans, which are readily available at stores and kiosks across the city.

Roaming charges: Before your journey, check with your mobile operator to see whether international roaming costs apply.
Depending on your plan, using data while overseas may result in extra expenses.

Healthcare And Medical Services
Maintaining your health on your travels is critical.
Here's all you should know about medical services in Trieste.

Health insurance
Consider purchasing travel insurance to cover medical emergencies, vacation cancellations, and lost possessions.
Check that your policy covers medical bills overseas.
EU citizens should carry their European Health Insurance Card (EHIC).

This card allows you to receive vital healthcare treatments in Italy at a reduced rate.
Trieste's hospitals and clinics, including as Ospedale di Cattinara and Ospedale Maggiore, provide emergency and general healthcare services.

Pharmacies (farmacie) are widely available throughout the city.
They sell over-the-counter drugs and offer assistance for minor health concerns.
Look for the green cross emblem to identify pharmacies.

Emergency Medical Services
In the event of a medical emergency, call 118 for an ambulance.
Hospitals and clinics have emergency equipment and English-speaking staff.
Keep these practical recommendations in mind as you plan your trip to Trieste.

Understanding currencies and payments, as well as how to communicate and obtain healthcare, will allow you to have a worry-free and fulfilling trip in this interesting city. Safe travels!

CHAPTER 8

Do's and Don'ts of Trieste

Understanding the local culture and customs is vital for having a positive time in Trieste.

This chapter discusses proper etiquette, social traditions, frequent mistakes to avoid, and local rules and regulations.

Following these guidelines will help you manage your stay successfully and politely.

Cultural Etiquette

Trieste has a complex cultural tapestry shaped by its eclectic history and fusion of Italian, Slovenian, and Austrian culture. Here are some important considerations to bear in mind:

Greetings
Formal greetings: In formal settings, a handshake is the usual greeting.
Use "Buongiorno" (Good morning) or "Buonasera" (Good evening) to welcome individuals, particularly in business settings.

When meeting someone for the first time, it is courteous to address them by title (e.g., Signore or Signora).

Kissing on both cheeks is a typical greeting amongst friends and relatives.
Wait for the other person to begin this gesture, which varies depending on familiarity.

Dress Code:
Smart Casual: Triestinians want to dress elegantly yet comfortably.
When dining at fancier restaurants or attending events, dress smart casual.

Outside of coastal locations, avoid wearing extremely casual attire such as flip-flops or beachwear.

Dress modestly while visiting religious locations, including churches.
For women, this includes covering their shoulders and knees. Men should not wear sleeveless shirts.

Table manners
Dining Etiquette: When dining, wait until the host invites you to begin eating. Keep your hands on the table (but not your elbows!) and use utensils for all foods, even pizza.

During toasting, make eye contact and exclaim "Salute!" (Cheers).
It is usual to toast each member at the table.
Understanding social traditions helps improve interactions with natives.

Punctuality is highly valued in Trieste, particularly during business meetings and social events.
If you are running late, please notify your host.

Coffee Culture

Rituals: Coffee is an important component of daily life in Trieste. Locals usually drink their coffee standing at the bar, and ordering a cappuccino after 11 a.m. is regarded odd.

Try to follow suit and embrace this local tradition.

Tipping: While not required, gratuities are appreciated.
In restaurants, it is typical to round up the bill or leave little change. For taxis, round up to the closest euro.

Common Mistakes To Avoid

Knowing frequent faux pas might help you fit in easily.
Speaking too loudly.

Italians are known for their expressive speech, yet speaking loudly in public places might attract unwelcome attention.

Keep your voice reasonable, especially in calmer settings such as cafés and churches.

Ignoring local customs: Failure to follow local customs may be viewed as disrespectful.
For example, entering a church with loud music or wearing unsuitable dress may insult residents.

Italians often eat dinner late, starting about 8 PM. Arriving at a restaurant too early may result in it being empty, causing you to lose out on the colorful evening scene.

Local Laws And Regulations
Understanding local laws can help prevent unintended breaches.
Alcohol and Public Behavior

Drinking laws: Italy's legal drinking age is 18. While drinking alcohol in public places is typically acceptable, public drunkenness can result in fines. Drink responsibly and show respect for your environment.

Environmental Responsibility: Littering is prohibited and can result in fines.
To dispose of rubbish, use specified waste containers.
Trieste takes pride in its cleanliness, and any contribution to this endeavor is welcomed.

Smoking regulations restrict smoking in enclosed public locations, such as restaurants and public transportation.
Look for approved smoking spots outside establishments.

Navigating Tourist Traps
While Trieste is less touristic than other Italian towns, you should still be wary of frequent tourist traps.

Popular tourist areas
Beware of expensive Souvenirs: In high-traffic places like Piazza Unità d'Italia, avoid stores selling expensive souvenirs.
Look for locally owned artisan businesses to obtain original presents at reasonable costs.

Tips for Restaurant Selection:
Avoid touristy restaurants.
Restaurants near big sites frequently cater to visitors, which results in higher pricing and lower-quality cuisine.
For a more genuine gastronomic experience, seek out local-favorite restaurants.

Guided Tours
Research Tours: While guided tours might enhance your experience, you should be cautious about the ones you choose.
Look for trusted providers with good reviews.
Avoid using forceful sales practices that are common in crowded locations.

When to Visit Attractions: Timing is Key.
Popular attractions may become packed during peak hours. Visiting early in the morning or late in the afternoon allows you to appreciate attractions such as Miramare Castle and the Roman Theatre with less tourists.

By following these guidelines, you will be able to navigate Trieste's cultural environment with ease and respect.
Understanding local customs and etiquette enhances your travel experience while also fostering important ties with the locals you encounter along the road.

Enjoy your adventure in this stunning city!

CHAPTER 9

Itinerary for All Travelers

Trieste has a wide range of experiences, making it an attractive destination for a variety of tourists.

Whether you are searching for a fast weekend getaway, a thorough dive into local culture, or an outdoor adventure, this chapter has itineraries suited to your preferences.

Each itinerary contains significant sites, eating recommendations, and ideas for making the most of your visit to this delightful city.

Weekend Getaway

For those with limited time in Trieste, this itinerary will help you maximize your trip by seeing the attractions and appreciating the local character.

DAY 01

Arrival and Exploration

Morning:
-Check into your hotel.
-For added convenience, consider lodging near Piazza Unità d'Italia or the Grand Canal.
-Caffè degli Specchi offers a classic Italian breakfast to start the day.
-Enjoy a coffee and a slice of strudel while taking in the breathtaking views of the plaza.

Mid-Morning: Explore Piazza Unità d'Italia, one of Europe's largest seashore squares.
-Take in the spectacular buildings, especially the Town
-Hall, as well as the stunning views of the sea.

For a substantial lunch, visit Trattoria Da Giovanni, a local favorite. Try Jota, a classic soup prepared with beans, sauerkraut, and pig.

Afternoon activities include seeing Miramare Castle, a beautiful castle built for Archduke Ferdinand Maximilian, which may be reached by bus or walking along the shore. -Explore the gardens and see the stunning views of the Adriatic Sea.

Evening activities include dinner at Osteria da Marino, where guests may enjoy traditional local food.
-Choose fresh seafood meals and match with local wines.
-Take an evening stroll along the Grand Canal, appreciating the beautiful buildings and bustling ambiance.

DAY 02

Culture and Relaxation

Morning activities include seeing the Roman Theatre, an old site.
-Explore the remains and envision the past acts that took place here.

Mid-morning:
-Visit Trieste's cathedral, located on the San Giusto hill.
-The breathtaking mosaics and panoramic vistas of the city are must-sees.

For lunch, visit Caffè Tommaseo, one of Trieste's oldest cafés, where you may relax with a small meal and local pastry.

Afternoon activities include visiting Museo Revoltella, which showcases modern art.
-The building itself is a piece of art, and the shows frequently feature both local and foreign artists.

Evening activities include dinner at La Tecia, where guests may enjoy regional dishes in a relaxed setting.
-Make sure to try some local wines to accompany your dinner.
-Finish your weekend with a glass of wine at a local wine bar and enjoy the calm atmosphere.

Cultural Immersion

This tour is meant to help guests better understand and appreciate Trieste's rich history and culture.

History and Artistic Exploration

DAY 01

Morning:
-Visit Piazza Unità d'Italia, the city's renowned plaza, to immerse yourself in its history and ambiance.

Mid-Morning:
-Visit Palazzo Pretorio, the former town hall with stunning architecture.
-Do not miss the nearby Church of Santa Maria Maggiore.

Lunch: Trattoria Al Pescatore offers fresh fish dishes inspired by the city's nautical heritage.

Afternoon: Visit the Museo di Storia Naturale to learn about the region's natural history.
-The museum's numerous displays present information on Trieste's biological surroundings.

Evening activities include dinner at Antica Trattoria Suban, where guests may enjoy local food in a historic setting.
-Do not miss the Gnocchi di Ricotta and Crespelle.
-Night activities include seeing a performance at the Teatro Lirico Giuseppe Verdi, a traditional Triestine venue for opera or classical music.

DAY 02

Local Life and Traditions

Morning visit to Mercato di Trieste, a lively market. Taste local cheeses, cured meats, and fresh veggies, and talk to the sellers about their offerings.

Mid-Morning:
-Visit the Synagogue of Trieste, a stunning edifice reflecting the city's Jewish past.
-Take a guided tour to discover its history and significance.

Lunch at Bottega del Caffè, where you may experience
-Trieste's famed coffee while enjoying a small meal.

Afternoon activities include seeing the museum at San Giusto Castle and Cathedral, as well as climbing to the summit for panoramic views.
-The cathedral's stunning mosaics are particularly worth seeing.

Evening activities include dinner at Ristorante Al Bagatto, where guests may enjoy authentic Triestine food.
-Try Sgombro (mackerel) and end with a local dessert.

DAY 03

Embrace the Arts

Morning:
Visit Museo Revoltella to explore modern art and learn about the city's creative evolution.

For lunch, choose Caffè Culturale, a quaint literary-themed restaurant ideal for a meal and a nice book.

Afternoon activity:
-Attend a local art or cuisine session to learn about Trieste culture firsthand.
-This is an excellent chance to meet the people and learn more about their way of life.

Evening activities include a guided wine tasting excursion to wrap up your cultural experience.
-Sample local wines while learning about their production and importance in the region.

Outdoor Adventure

Trieste has stunning landscapes, hiking paths, and seaside experiences to offer nature lovers and adventurers. This program is designed for individuals who wish to experience the great outdoors.

Coastal and Scenic Adventures

DAY 01

Morning:
-Begin your morning journey in Miramar Castle and Park, known for its spectacular architecture and expansive grounds.
-Take the time to go around the seashore walks.
-Pack a picnic lunch and enjoy the breathtaking views of the castle's surrounding grounds.

Afternoon activity:
-Hike along the Trieste coastline near the castle.
-The Sentiero Rilke is a famous beachfront route that offers beautiful views of the Adriatic Sea and surrounding rocks.

Evening plans include dinner at Ristorante La Cantina to unwind after a day of exploration.
-The fish is fresh and tasty.

Nature and Exploration

DAY 02

Morning:
-Spend the morning trekking in the picturesque Val Rosandra Nature Reserve, located just outside the city.
-The routes range in difficulty and provide breathtaking views of the valley and adjacent hills.

Lunch:
-Visit a nearby agriturismo for a farm-to-table lunch including local food and handcrafted delights.

Afternoon activity: Explore the ruins of the old aqueduct in the natural reserve.
-This historical landmark is surrounded by nature.

Evening
-Trattoria La Caverna offers classic food in a rustic environment.
-The outside sitting enhances the mood after a day of trekking.

DAY 03 **Water Activities & Relaxation**

Morning:
-Activities include a lovely boat excursion to Muggia, a charming village located south of Trieste.
-Enjoy the beauty of the shoreline from the ocean.

Lunch:
-Seaside Lunch in Muggia: Dine at a waterfront restaurant and sample local seafood while admiring the picturesque port.

Afternoon activities include renting a kayak to explore the coast or relaxing on the beach and swimming in the Adriatic sea.

Evening
-Enjoy a goodbye supper at a restaurant in Trieste, with local wines and traditional foods, to mark the conclusion of your adventurous visit.

Family-Friendly Trip

Traveling with your family can be a pleasant trip, and Trieste has a wide range of sights and activities for all ages.
Here's a proposed agenda that will keep everyone occupied.

Arrival and Exploration

DAY 01

Morning:
-Check in to a family-friendly hotel, such as the NH Trieste, with big rooms and a central location.
Caffè Tommaseo offers a substantial breakfast with local pastries.
-The café provides a pleasant ambiance, which is ideal for families.

Mid-Morning:
-Begin your journey in Piazza Unità d'Italia, Europe's largest seafront square.
-Children may run about while parents admire the gorgeous building.

-For lunch, try Trattoria Da Giovanni, a family-friendly restaurant that offers wonderful local food.
-The calm setting is ideal for children, and the food offers something for everyone.

Afternoon activities include visiting Miramare Castle and seeing its gardens and grounds.
-The castle itself is remarkable, and a guided tour will teach you about its history.

Dinner at Pizza & Co. is a family favorite due to its informal atmosphere and many pizza selections.
-Kids will enjoy selecting their toppings.

Fun and Learning

DAY 02

Morning activities at Trieste Science Center include interactive experiences.
-The hands-on exhibits are ideal for inquiring minds and provide enjoyable learning opportunities.

Lunch at Caffè Culturale, a charming café serving light meals and sweets.
-It is an excellent place to refuel before your next excursion.

Afternoon:
-Visit the Trieste Aquarium.
-It is modest yet quite interesting for children, exhibiting local aquatic life.

Evening plans include dinner at Ristorante Al Bagatto, which offers a cuisine suitable for both adults and children.
-Try the local fish or let the kids eat pasta dishes.

DAY 03

Nature and Adventure

Morning activity:
-Visit Val Rosandra Nature Reserve for a scenic trek with your family.
-Choose an easy path that is appropriate for all ages.
-The environment is stunning, providing for an excellent outdoor experience.

Lunch:
-Pack a picnic to enjoy in the wildlife reserve. This is an excellent way to unwind and take in the stunning scenery.

After lunch, explore the Old Aqueduct Ruins. Children may tour the place and learn about its historical significance.

Evening:
-Return to Trieste and dine at La Tecia. The relaxed environment is ideal for families, and the menu includes a range of local delicacies.

DAY 04

Relaxation and departure

Morning activities include a boat ride to Muggia, a neighboring village.
-The boat voyage itself is an experience for children.

Lunch at a Waterfront Restaurant: Enjoy a lunch with a view of the water.
-Muggia boasts lovely areas ideal for families.
Spend the afternoon at Muggia's beach.
-Children may play on the beach and swim, allowing for a calm way to end the trip.

Evening: Return to Trieste and have a final meal before departing.

Budget Travel

Traveling on a budget in Trieste does not imply losing excellent experiences. Here's how to explore the city without breaking the bank.

Discovering Trieste

DAY 01

For affordable lodgings, choose Hotel Istria or hostels that provide shared and private rooms at low costs.
Breakfast at a Local Bakery:
-Get a croissant and coffee for a few euros.

Mid-Morning:
Piazza Unità d'Italia: Enjoy the views without spending money.

Lunch:
-Grab a panino or tramezzino from a nearby deli.
-These sandwiches are inexpensive and satisfying.

Afternoon activities include visiting free attractions such as the Roman Theatre and San Giusto Castle, which require little or no admission costs.
-The views from the castle are well worth the climb.

Evening:
-Dinner at a Local Pizzeria: Grab a slice of pizza.
-Many restaurants have "al taglio" (by the slice) alternatives, which are ideal for budget tourists.

Culture and History

DAY 02

Morning:
-Join a free walking tour in Trieste.
-These tours are tip-based, so you may pay what you can afford while learning about the city's history.

Lunch
 Picnic Lunch: Purchase goods from a nearby grocery or market and have a picnic at a park, such as the Giardini Pubblici.

Afternoon:
-Research museums that provide free admittance on specified days.
-The Museo Revoltella sometimes offers free days, and the Museo di Storia Naturale is also reasonably priced.

Evening activities include dinner at a local trattoria with daily specialties. Many provide cheap set dinners with many courses.

DAY 03

Enjoy the outdoors and scenery

Morning:
-Spend the day hiking in Val Rosandra.
-It is free and provides breathtaking views and natural walks.
-Bring a lunch to eat while exploring.

Lunch:
-Bring your own packed lunch and enjoy the wonderful surroundings.

Afternoon activity:
-Visit local markets for fresh vegetables, reasonable snacks, and unusual items without spending much.

Evening:
-Find an economical local osteria that serves basic yet tasty dishes.

DAY 04

Relaxation and departure

Morning:
-Take a boat to Muggia for a low cost.
-Enjoy the gorgeous ride.

For lunch, Muggia offers affordable waterfront dining options.
-Enjoy local fish on a budget.

Afternoon activities include sunbathing and swimming on the beach.
-This is a calm and free approach to enjoy the beach.

Evening:
-Enjoy a final dinner in Trieste with happy hour offers at pubs and restaurants.

Solo Traveler's Guide

Solo travel provides you opportunity to explore at your own speed.
Here is a suggested itinerary for solitary tourists seeking to explore Trieste.

Arrival and Initial Exploration

DAY 01

Morning itinerary:
-Check-in at Hostel Gallo or a budget hotel in the city center.
Breakfast at Caffè Tommaseo, a historic café with great people-watching opportunities.

Mid-Morning:
-Explore Piazza Unità d'Italia, take photographs, and enjoy the lively environment.
-For lunch, visit a café and sample a local sandwich or pastry.

Afternoon:
-Join a free walking tour to meet other visitors and learn about Trieste's history with a qualified guide.

Evening activities include a meal at a local osteria to connect with the community.
-Choose a restaurant recognized for its collaborative eating experience.

Culture and Connection

DAY 02

Morning:
-Visit Museo Revoltella, a modern art museum with current works reflecting the city's culture.
-Choose a café with free Wi-Fi for lunch to relax, check messages, and plan your next activities.

Spend the afternoon at the Roman Theatre.
-The place is rich in history and provides a tranquil setting for introspection.

Evening activities include attending local events such as music, theater, or culture.
-Engaging with locals and other tourists can result in important connections.

DAY 03

Nature and solitude

Morning activities include hiking in Val Rosandra to spend time with nature.
-Bring a small lunch and enjoy the serenity of the trails.

Lunch options include a picnic in the park or a lovely location to eat your packed lunch.

Afternoon:
-Explore the Nature Reserve, taking time to relax and contemplate.

Evening:
supper at a Cozy Restaurant:
-Enjoy a relaxing supper at a restaurant noted for its environment and delicious food.

DAY 04

Leisure and Reflection

Morning:
-Ferry to Muggia:
-Enjoy a relaxing ferry trip to Muggia. Relax and enjoy the views from the boat.

Lunch by the Sea:
-Relax with a relaxed meal at a seaside café in Muggia, taking in the wonderful surroundings.

Afternoon:
-Explore Muggia's picturesque streets and appreciate the slower pace.

Evening:
-Return to Trieste for a final meal.
-Choose a relaxed eatery where you may reflect on your travels.

Romantic Getaways

Trieste provides a beautiful setting for couples seeking to relax and enjoy each other's company. This itinerary focuses on romantic experiences.

Arrival and Romance

DAY 01

Morning:
-Check-in to a lovely hotel, such as Savoia Excelsior Palace, or a charming boutique hotel.
-Start your holiday with breakfast at Caffè degli Specchi, which overlooks Piazza Unità d'Italia.

Mid-Morning:
-Stroll Through the City:
-Experience the gorgeous streets and ambiance.
- For one-of-a-kind items, visit artisan stores.

Lunch at a Scenic Café: Enjoy a simple meal with outside sitting and people-watching.

Afternoon:
-Visit Miramar Castle and its stunning grounds.
- Stroll hand in hand along the beach pathways, taking in the breathtaking sights.

Evening activities include a romantic meal at Ristorante Al Bagatto, featuring local delicacies.
-Consider sharing many meals to create a gourmet experience.

Culture and Connection

DAY 02

Morning activity:
-Visit San Giusto Cathedral and enjoy the quiet ambiance.
Lunch:
-At Caffè Culturale, enjoy a pleasant meal and share your finest travel memories.

Afternoon:
-Visit Museo Revoltella to explore modern art together.
-Discuss the pieces that speak to you both.

In the evening, consider attending a local music or show.
-Enjoying live music together might result in amazing experiences.

Nature and Relaxation

DAY 03

Morning activity:
-Hike through Val Rosandra nature reserve.

Lunch
-Picnic Lunch:
-Prepare a romantic picnic to eat in a lovely location.

Afternoon activities include exploring the remnants of the Old Aqueduct, which have historical importance and spectacular vistas.

Evening:
-Visit Vittoria Lighthouse for a stunning sunset view.
-It is an ideal romantic location.

Final Relaxation and Departure

DAY 04

Morning:
-Take a leisurely boat trip to Muggia and enjoy the scenery together.

Lunch at a Waterfront Restaurant:
-Treat yourself to a romantic dinner with stunning sea views.

Afternoon activities include a stroll through Muggia, where you may stop at stores and spend time together.

Evening:
-Return to Trieste for a farewell dinner.
-Choose a particular restaurant for your final evening together, toasting to your unforgettable vacation.

These itineraries appeal to families, budget travelers, solitary explorers, and couples, guaranteeing that every tourist may discover the perfect experience in Trieste.

Trieste, with its mix of history, culture, and natural beauty, has something for everyone.
Enjoy your adventure!

CHAPTER 10

Trieste on a Budget

Trieste, with its gorgeous architecture, vibrant culture, and rich history, is more than just a luxury destination.

It provides a wide range of experiences that are reasonably priced.

This chapter looks at how to enjoy Trieste while staying within your budget, including free attractions, low-cost food alternatives, budget-friendly lodging, and transit advice.

Free Or Inexpensive Attractions

Trieste has several free or inexpensive attractions.
Here are a few highlights to consider:

Piazza Unità d'Italia
Piazza Unità d'Italia, one of Europe's largest seafront squares, is a must-see.
The area is surrounded by exquisite neoclassical structures and has spectacular views of the Adriatic Sea.

Simply walking around and taking in the ambiance is free.

San Giusto Castle
San Giusto Castle is another popular sight that charges only a nominal admission price.
Climbing to the castle provides panoramic views of the city and neighboring landscapes.

The historical value and well-preserved architecture justify the minimal expenditure.

Roman Theater
The Roman Theatre, located in the city center, is a fascinating reminder of Trieste's historic history.

Access to the site is free, and it is a good place to learn about the city's history while relaxing amid the ruins.

The Grand Canal
Strolling around the Canal Grande allows you to see beautiful structures and bustling cafes.

The atmosphere is particularly appealing in the evening, when the lights reflect off the sea.

This lovely stroll is completely free and ideal for capturing photographs.

Val Rosandra Nature Reserve.
If you enjoy nature, Val Rosandra is a must-see.
The reserve has lovely hiking paths, abundant flora, and breathtaking rock formations.

Exploring the region is free and offers a wonderful retreat from the city.

Museums with Free Admission Days
Many museums in Trieste, including the Museo Revoltella and the Museo di Storia Naturale, provide free entry on certain days.

Plan your vacation to coincide with these dates to take advantage of free access to these cultural institutions.

Cost-Effective Dining
Eating out in Trieste may be inexpensive with a little forethought.
Here are some possibilities for cost-effective dining:

Tramezzini & Street Food
Tramezzini, triangular sandwiches packed with a variety of toppings, are a favorite snack in Trieste.

Many local cafés and taverns sell them for a few euros.
They make for a quick, delicious, and inexpensive supper.

Local bakeries
Trieste has many bakeries where you can get fresh pastries or pizza by the slice.

Try the local favorites, pizzette (small pizzas) and crostini (toasted bread with toppings). These solutions are both satisfying and inexpensive.

Tavola Calde
Tavole calde are cafes that offer hot meals at low costs.
You may get daily specials such pasta, meat meals, and side dishes.
These establishments are frequently visited by locals, providing a real eating experience without the tourist markup.

Budget Restaurants
Look for restaurants that serve a "menu del giorno" (menu of the day), which usually includes an appetizer, main dish, and occasionally dessert for a set fee.

Restaurants such as Osteria Al Bagatto and Trattoria Da Giovanni serve delicious meals at cheap pricing.

Cafés and bars.
Drinking a coffee or a glass of local wine at one of Trieste's many cafés may also be inexpensive. Many locations have aperitivo offers, which allow you to enjoy a drink and small appetizers for a reasonable price.

Low-cost Accommodation Options
Finding economical lodging in Trieste is simpler than you would expect.
Here are some choices to consider:

Hostels
Hostels like Hostel Gallo and Cooee provide affordable dormitory and individual room alternatives.

Staying at a hostel may be an excellent chance to meet other travelers and share stories.

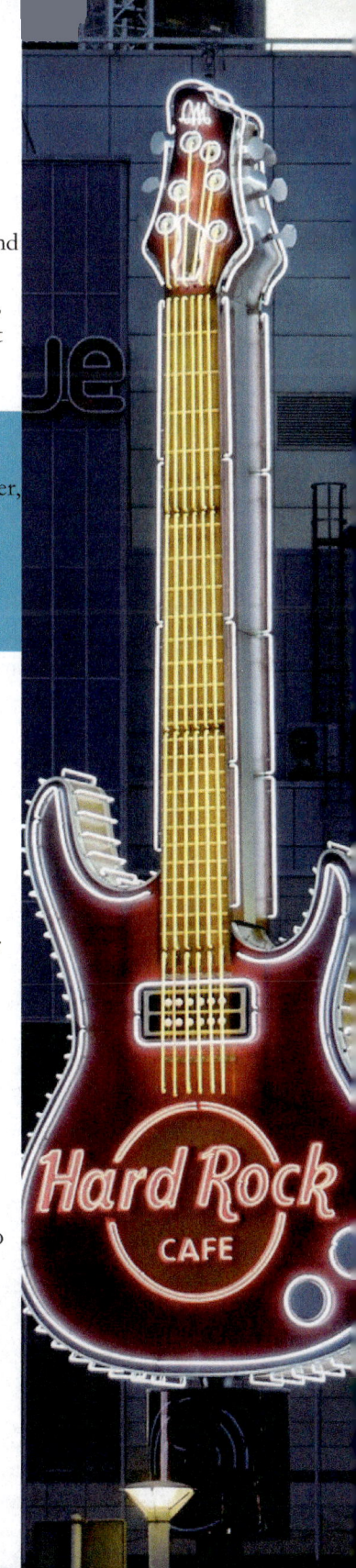

Guest homes and bed and breakfasts

Consider guesthouses or bed-and-breakfasts for a more comfortable stay at a lesser cost than hotels.

Places like B&B La Storia and Albergo Garni Ristorante frequently have a pleasant atmosphere and provide breakfast in the hotel fee.

Budget Hotels

There are various cheap hotels in Trieste, such as Hotel Italia and Hotel Istria, that provide pleasant lodgings at moderate prices.

Look for specials and book ahead of time to get the best pricing.

Short-term rentals

Platforms such as Airbnb and local rental sites might provide homes or rooms at cheap prices, especially if you are traveling in groups.

This option may include cooking facilities, allowing you to make certain meals while saving money on dining out.

Ways To Save On Transportation

Transportation costs might mount up, but there are lots of ways to save while traveling around Trieste:

Walking.
Many of Trieste's attractions are within walking distance of one another.
Walking allows you to experience the city's beauty while discovering hidden jewels along the route.
The pedestrian-friendly layout allows for simple exploration.

Public transportation.
Trieste has an effective public transportation system that includes buses and trams.
A single ticket is reasonably priced, and you can purchase a day pass for unlimited rides.
This is a good way to get to sights further out from the city center.

Biking
Consider hiring a bicycle to explore the city and its surroundings. Trieste is becoming more bicycle-friendly, and cycling allows you to see more while enjoying the outdoors.
Look for rental stores that provide daily pricing.

Car Rental
If you want to go outside Trieste, consider hiring a car.
Look for low-cost rental providers and reserve ahead of time to obtain the greatest deal.
This might be a cost-effective option to visit local sites such as the beach village of Muggia or the picturesque hills of the Collio Wine Region.

Ferries to nearby towns.
If you want to see surrounding coastal towns, ferries are a gorgeous and frequently inexpensive method to travel.
The boat from Trieste to Muggia is a fantastic choice that offers stunning views of the shore.

With careful planning and a little innovation, you can enjoy Trieste on a budget.
From free sights to low-cost food and lodging, you can enjoy the beauty of this city without breaking the bank.

Embrace the local culture, relish the cuisine, and enjoy the stunning sights —all while staying within your budget.

CHAPTER 11

Exploring Trieste's surroundings

Trieste's unusual geographical location at the crossroads of Italy, Slovenia, and Croatia gives it an excellent starting point for seeing a variety of breathtaking landscapes and rich cultural attractions.

Whether you are looking for historical monuments, wine routes, or calm beach vacations, the neighboring locations provide plenty of possibilities.

This chapter discusses the greatest day trips and excursions from Trieste, allowing you to see the wonderful places around.

Day Trips In Slovenia And Croatia

A. Piran, Slovenia.
The seaside village of Piran, located just a short drive or bus trip from Trieste, is a must-see. Piran, with its small alleyways, historic buildings, and breathtaking vistas of the Adriatic Sea, seems like a slice of Italy with a Slavic touch.

To do:
Visit Tartini Square, named for renowned musician Giuseppe Tartini.

Visit the Church of St. George for stunning views of the town and sea.

Enjoy fresh seafood at a nearby restaurant.

Ljubljana, Slovenia
Ljubljana, Slovenia's capital city, is approximately 1.5 hours by car or bus from Trieste.

It is a great day travel destination, known for its lovely ancient town and dynamic cultural environment.

Activities include strolling along the Ljubljanica River and relaxing at riverfront cafés.

Explore the Ljubljana Castle's breathtaking vistas and fascinating exhibits.

Visit the Central Market to eat local products and purchase handcrafted gifts.

Rovinj, Croatia
For a taste of Croatia, visit Rovinj, a lovely beach town approximately two hours from Trieste.

The bustling old town is distinguished by its cobblestone streets and colorful houses.

Things to do:
Walk through the small lanes to St. Euphemia's Church for panoramic views.

Relax along the port and enjoy the view of fishing boats and cafés.

Try local specialties like shrimp risotto and fresh truffles at seaside eateries.

Karst Region And Wine Routes
Explore the Karst Region
The Karst area, noted for its distinctive limestone landscapes and stunning caverns, is located just northwest of Trieste.

This location is known for its natural beauty and provides a variety of outdoor activities.

To do:
Visit the UNESCO World Heritage site, Škocjan Caves, known for its subterranean canyons and waterfalls.
Guided tours explain the geological significance of the caverns.
Explore Postojna Cave, one of the world's largest karst caverns, with a train journey through its remarkable rock formations.

Wine Routes
The Karst area is well known for its wine production, especially Teran and Refošk.
Take a wine tour to sample local varietals and see the lovely vineyards.

Wine Routes:
Explore local wineries like Vinakras or Klet Brda, where you may sample wines coupled with regional cuisine.
Take vineyard excursions to learn about the winemaking process and purchase bottles directly from the growers.

Beach Getaways Near Trieste

Sistiana.
Sistiana, located only a short drive from Trieste, is known for its gorgeous beaches and blue seas.

It is ideal for a day spent sunbathing, swimming, or simply resting by the sea.

Activities:
Rent sun loungers and umbrellas at Sistiana Bay for a relaxing day.
Enjoy an active day at the beach with water sports like kayaking or paddleboarding.

Grado
Grado, sometimes known as the "Island of the Sun," is home to extensive sandy beaches and a picturesque medieval town.

It is roughly an hour from Trieste and perfect for families.

To do:
Enjoy the beach at Spiaggia Costa Azzurra, ideal for families with shallow waters.

Explore the ancient town, with picturesque alleys, shops, and the Basilica di Sant'Eufemia.

Lignano Sabbiadoro
For those prepared to venture a little further, Lignano Sabbiadoro has wide sandy beaches, water parks, and a lively nightlife.

It is located around 1.5 hours from Trieste and is a renowned tourist attraction.

Things to do:
Relax on the beach or try water sports.
Visit Aquasplash, a water park suitable for both families and adrenaline seekers.

Castles And Historic Sites Outside Of The City

Miramare Castle
Miramare fortress, located near Trieste, is a beautiful 19th-century fortress on the seafront.
It was erected for Archduke Ferdinand Maximilian of Austria and features lovely gardens.

Activities include seeing the castle's sumptuous chambers with original furniture, as well as strolling around the adjacent park with exotic flora and stunning sea views.

Castello di Duino
Castello di Duino is located further along the shore, positioned on a rock overlooking the Adriatic Sea. The castle has a long history, reaching back to the 14th century, and provides an intriguing view into noble life.

Things to do:
Take a guided tour to learn about the castle's history and significance in historical events.
Explore the Rilke Path, a picturesque walk with breathtaking coastal views.

The Abbey of St. Mary of Aquileia
Aquileia, located around 90 minutes from Trieste, was once one of the Roman Empire's most significant cities.

Today, the remains of the Basilica di Aquileia, a UNESCO World Heritage site, bear witness to its historical significance.

Activities include visiting the basilica to see the well-preserved Roman mosaics and exploring the archeological region, which includes vestiges of Roman structures and the ancient forum.

Castle of San Giusto

Within Trieste, Castello di San Giusto provides a historical viewpoint as well as stunning views of the city.

This fortress, built in the 15th century, may be found atop the San Giusto hill.

Things to Do:

Visit the castle museum to learn about Trieste's history via artifacts. Enjoy panoramic views of Trieste from the castle's towers, ideal for photography.

Exploring the surrounds of Trieste provides a wealth of experiences. From the seaside beauties of Slovenia and Croatia to the breathtaking scenery of the Karst area, there is something for every sort of traveller.

Whether you are tasting local wines, relaxing on sun-kissed beaches, or seeing centuries-old castles, these excursions will enrich your travel and leave you with lasting memories of this lovely area of Europe.

CHAPTER 12

Art and Culture in Trieste

Trieste is more than simply a stunning seaside city; it is also a thriving center of arts and culture.

Trieste, with its rich history, many influences, and vibrant creative environment, provides a wealth of experiences for art, theater, and literature fans.

This chapter explores the numerous aspects of Trieste's cultural environment, focusing on theaters, museums, yearly events, and the city's literary past.

Theater And Performance Venues

Trieste has a lively theatrical culture, with facilities catering to a variety of creative expressions, including opera and contemporary plays.

Teatro Lirico Giuseppe Verdi.
The Teatro Lirico Giuseppe Verdi, an opera building built in 1801, is one of Trieste's cultural highlights.

This facility, known for its beautiful neoclassical design, accommodates a diverse range of productions, including opera, ballet, and classical concerts.

Expect major opera performances by famous companies, involving local and international artists.

Participate in periodic festivals including classical and contemporary pieces, showcasing both rising and experienced performers.

Teatro Miela
Teatro Miela is another popular venue that specializes in experimental theater and contemporary events.

Located in the center of the city, this tiny room frequently showcases works that challenge standard narrative.

Expect to see a variety of performances, such as plays, dance, and music, including local artists and unique creations.

Participate in seminars and conversations to promote cultural discourse in the neighborhood.

Theatre Festivals
Trieste also hosts various theatrical events, notably the Trieste Science+Fiction Festival, which focuses on science fiction and fantasy genres.

This festival gathers filmmakers and viewers from all over the world, displaying creative works and giving a forum for conversations about the future of cinema.

Museum And Galleries
The city's museums and galleries represent its diverse cultural heritage, displaying both historical items and current artwork.

Museum Revoltella
The Museo Revoltella is dedicated to modern art and has an exceptional collection from the nineteenth and twentieth centuries.

This museum not only displays paintings and sculptures, but it also offers temporary exhibits by modern artists.

Expect to explore works by prominent artists, including those from the Italian avant-garde movement. Attend seminars and guided tours to understand the significance of the artworks on show.

Museo Di Storia Naturale
For individuals interested in natural history, the Museo di Storia Naturale has intriguing displays ranging from geology to paleontology.

The museum's holdings contain a wide range of items that show the region's biodiversity.

Expect interactive displays that interest visitors of all ages, making it a terrific location for families.

Additionally, participate in educational activities to promote an awareness for wildlife and conservation.

Contemporary Art Galleries.
In addition to established museums, Trieste is home to various contemporary art galleries, such as Galleria Templon and Galleria d'Arte Moderna, which feature rotating exhibitions from both local and international artists, providing an opportunity to experience Trieste's cutting-edge art scene.

Trieste Film Festival & Other Events
Trieste organizes a variety of film and cultural festivals throughout the year to celebrate the arts in all of their manifestations.

Trieste Film Festival.
The Trieste Film Festival, held in January, is a highlight of the cultural calendar.
This festival focuses on films from Central and Eastern Europe, providing a forum for both budding filmmakers and recognized artists.

Expect screenings of feature films, documentaries, and shorts featuring varied cinematic voices from the area.
Interact with filmmakers, attend seminars, and network at events.

B. Other cultural festivals.
Aside from the film festival, Trieste holds various other events, including the Trieste Science+Fiction Festival and the Trieste Music Festival.
Each event highlights a distinct facet of the city's cultural identity, ranging from science fiction films to classical music concerts.

Literary Trieste: Exploring Its Famous Writers

Trieste has a long literary history, having produced numerous renowned writers whose works were influenced by the city's vibrant cultural scene.

James Joyce

One of the most well-known literary characters linked with Trieste is James Joyce.

The famed author of "Ulysses" resided in the city for many years and was inspired by its dynamic environment.

Visitors may tour various Joyce-related locales, including the Caffè Tommaseo, where he frequently wrote and socialized.

Explore:

The James Joyce Museum, housed at the author's home, provides insight into his life and works.

Explore Trieste through Joyce's eyes and consider how it inspired his writing.

Italo Svevo

Italo Svevo, another major literary personality, is well-known for his work "Zeno's Conscience," which delves into questions of identity and existentialism.

Svevo's art was heavily impacted by the heterogeneous setting of Trieste.

Explore areas in Trieste that inspired Svevo, such as his old house and local cafés where he met with other writers and intellectuals.

Participate in literary events or debates that highlight Svevo's literary achievements and cultural background.

The Contemporary Literary Scene

Trieste's literary tradition lives on today, with a strong modern literary scene.
The city holds various literary festivals, book launches, and readings, making it a thriving community for both writers and readers.

Expect to engage with local authors and participate in seminars on writing skills and storytelling.
Explore independent bookshops with local and international writers to create a passion for literature in the community.

Trieste's artistic and cultural scene is as diverse as its historical influences.
From engaging theaters and museums to bustling festivals and literary icons, the city provides tourists with a diverse range of experiences.

Whether you are watching a play, visiting a museum, or learning about the city's literary ties, Trieste welcomes you to immerse yourself in its artistic essence.

Each encounter contributes to a better knowledge of this distinctive city and its role in Europe's cultural environment.

CHAPTER 13

Nightlife in Trieste

Trieste, with its breathtaking seaside vistas and rich cultural past, evolves into a thriving nightlife hotspot once the sun sets.

The city has a wide range of nighttime entertainment choices, from casual bars to vibrant clubs.

In this chapter, we will look at Trieste's eclectic nightlife culture, which includes popular pubs, drink places, music venues, and the allure of nocturnal strolls along the shore.

Bars And Pubs In Trieste

Traditional Italian bars.
Trieste has a lot of typical Italian pubs where you may have coffee during the day and switch to a bottle of wine or spritz in the evening.

Caffè Tommaseo is one such historical institution. Established in 1830, it is a historic icon and an excellent place to relax while sipping a local aperitif.

Expect a calm ambiance with wooden furnishings and outdoor dining. Enjoy local wines and classic Italian drinks, including the renowned spritz.

Local pubs
For a more relaxed atmosphere, visit local pubs such as The Irish Pub or Pub da Miki.
These establishments frequently provide a diverse selection of beers, both domestic and imported, and have a welcoming, relaxed atmosphere.

Expect pub quizzes and live sports screens, as well as a bustling social scene with both locals and visitors.

Uniquely Themed Bars
Trieste also features a few unusual themed pubs that are noteworthy for their originality.
For example, Caffè San Marco, a classic literary café, becomes a bar at night.

It provides a pleasant environment packed with literature and art, making it popular with individuals who want a more cerebral setting.

Cocktail And Wine Bars
Upscale Cocktail Bars
Trieste's cocktail industry is flourishing, with numerous establishments dedicated to creating one-of-a-kind and artisanal beverages.

Bistro 3 is one such establishment, noted for its inventive drinks made using locally sourced ingredients.

Expect:
A sophisticated atmosphere with professional mixologists dedicated about their trade.

Offering signature drinks with regional tastes and traditional alternatives.

Wine Bars.
Trieste is located near renowned wine areas, making wine bars popular among both locals and visitors.
Enoteca Sotto il Noce serves a large range of local wines, including the well-known Teran and Refosco kinds.

Expect a trained staff to assist you through samples.
Enjoy pairing wines with local cheeses and charcuterie for a full experience.

The Mediterranean Vibe
For a more casual atmosphere, visit Caffè degli Specchi in Piazza Unità d'Italia.

This exquisite café offers delectable drinks and wines while offering stunning views of the plaza, especially when the sun sets.

Nightclubs & Live Music Venues
Nightclubs
For those eager to dance the night away, Trieste has a few nightclubs to suit all preferences.
Cafè del Teatro is a popular pick, noted for its lively environment and wide music selections that range from house to pop.

Expect themed nights with guest DJs for a vibrant experience. The audience is trendy, and the dance floor fills up throughout the night.

Live Music Venues
Venues such as Teatro Miela and Circolo Controtempo cater to live music aficionados.
These venues routinely showcase local bands, foreign musicians, and open mic nights, offering a platform for budding talent.

Expect a combination of genres such as rock, jazz, and folk music, as well as an intimate atmosphere to engage with the artists.

Cultural Events

Trieste's nightlife includes more than simply clubs and pubs. Cultural activities such as poetry readings, art exhibitions, and theatrical performances take place in a variety of settings.

Check local listings for events at venues such as Teatro Lirico Giuseppe Verdi, where you could see a performance that carries the city's cultural mood into the evening.

Evening Walks On The Waterfront

Walking around Trieste's shoreline in the evening is one of the most wonderful ways to view the city at night.

The Canal Grande and Piazza Unità d'Italia are lovely backgrounds for a leisurely stroll, especially as the lights reflect on the water.

Canal Grande.

The Canal Grande, dotted with cafés and restaurants, is especially beautiful at night.

The beautiful sound of water lapping against the docks enhances the romantic scene.

Expect street entertainers and musicians to provide entertainment along the route.

Many places to enjoy gelato or drinks while admiring the vista.

The Waterfront Promenade

As you travel towards the Molo Audace, you will see panoramic views of the Adriatic Sea and the beautiful Castello di Miramare lighted up in the distance.

This location is ideal for taking great photos and enjoying the refreshing sea wind.

Expect breathtaking sunset views, particularly during warmer months.

Relax on the seats and enjoy the calm of the sea.

Night Markets and Festivals

Trieste features night markets and festivals at various periods of the year, which enhances the nightlife experience.

Local craftsmen and food sellers put up stalls around the shoreline, resulting in a lively environment with music, food, and crafts.

Expect to experience local specialties and homemade crafts, as well as a dynamic throng celebrating the city's joyful atmosphere.

Trieste's nightlife is a lovely mix of heritage and innovation that has something for everyone.

Whether you like drinking drinks at a classy bar, partying at a club, or listening to live music, the city has an enticing environment.

A night out in Trieste guarantees a wonderful experience, highlighting the city's distinct charm as it comes alive after dark.

Whether you are a native or a guest, Trieste's nightlife will make an impact.

CHAPTER 14

Shopping in Trieste

Trieste provides a distinctive shopping experience that reflects its rich cultural heritage and creative flare.

From quaint village markets to high-end stores, the city accommodates to a wide range of preferences and budgets.

In this chapter, we will look at the greatest shopping districts, local markets, specialist stores, and fashion boutiques in Trieste, giving you a full guide to making the most of your retail therapy in this stunning seaside city.

Best Shopping Streets
The Union Street
Via dell'Unione is one of Trieste's principal retail streets.
This busy boulevard is dotted with a variety of stores, cafés, and restaurants.

Local boutiques and worldwide brands are all available here, making it a popular destination for both locals and visitors.
Expect:

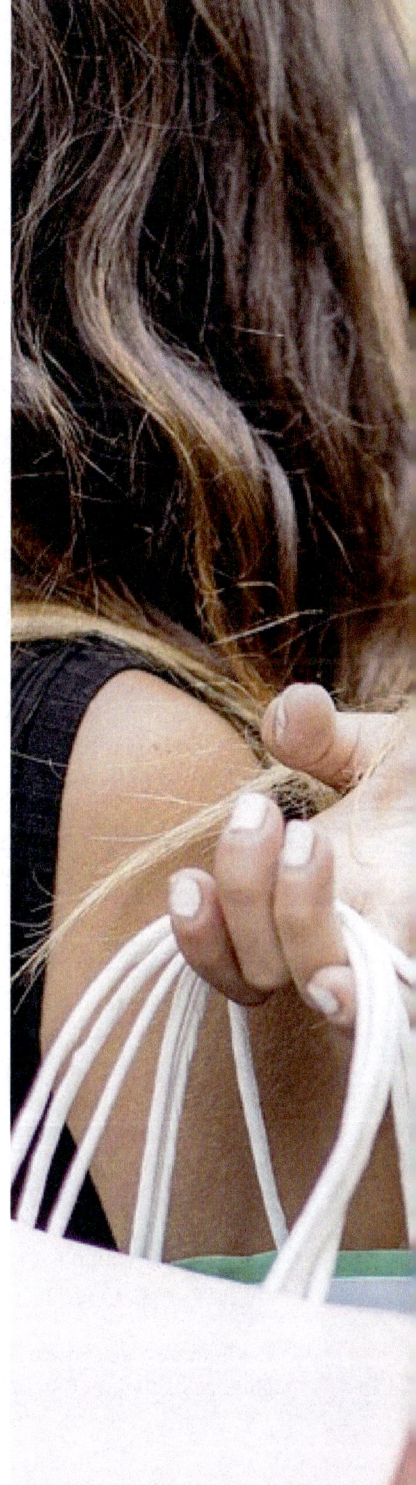

A bustling environment, especially on weekends when residents throng to the area.

A diverse range of shops for fashion and home items.

Corso Italia
Corso Italia is another popular shopping center, recognized for its diverse selection of retailers.

This street has a mix of high-street businesses and lovely local boutiques, offering a well-rounded shopping experience.

Expect seasonal sales and promotions at numerous retailers, with excellent deals.

Refuel with coffee or gelato at one of the numerous cafés while shopping.

Piazza della Borsa, located in the heart of the city, is a magnificent square and luxury retail destination.

The region is home to various high-end stores and luxury brands, making it an ideal destination for anyone seeking to indulge.

Expect to find elegant boutiques and a gorgeous location for a leisurely shopping experience.

Additionally, nearby cafés provide a glimpse of the old buildings.

Local Markets And Artisan Shops
Mercato Coperto
The Mercato Coperto, or Covered Market, is a must-see for those interested in local fruit, cheeses, and meats.

This lively market provides a sensory experience bursting with vivid colors and delectable fragrances.

Expect to find fresh, locally sourced items such as seasonal fruits and artisanal cheeses, as well as friendly merchants willing to offer their experience and advice.

Artisan Shops
Trieste has various artisan stores that highlight the city's great workmanship.

Places like Bottega dei Sapori provide handcrafted goods ranging from pottery to fabrics, allowing you to bring a piece of Trieste home with you.

Expect unique, one-of-a-kind objects that showcase local culture and creativity.

Meet craftsmen and learn their trade.
Flea Markets
If you like treasure hunting, visit the Flea Market in Piazza Vittorio Veneto. This market is open on weekends and is a terrific location to find vintage clothing, antiques, and unique knickknacks.

Expect a vibrant and eclectic setting full with hidden gems.
Local sellers offer bargaining possibilities, creating a unique purchasing experience.

Souvenir And Specialty Stores
Local Specialties
When it comes to souvenirs, Trieste offers an abundance of possibilities that express its own personality.

Look for local specialties such as coffee, notably from Caffè Illy, which is well-known for its quality.
Expect to receive nicely packaged specialty coffee blends suitable for gifts or personal usage.

Other gastronomic delights include local olive oil, wines, and desserts.

Gift Shops.
There are various gift stores in Trieste that sell a variety of gifts, including postcards and homemade products.
Souvenirs di Trieste is a popular store where you can buy souvenirs that embodies the soul of the city.

Expect to find a diverse selection of Trieste-themed things, such as pottery, magnets, and novels.
Additionally, there are items that highlight local art and culture, making them perfect for gifts or souvenirs.

Specialty Food Shop
Do not miss out on specialist food shops like Gastronomia Dalla Rosa, where you may get a wide range of gourmet items.

These establishments reflect the region's gastronomic tradition, offering cured meats and handmade cheeses.

Expect tastings and samples to discover the unique flavors of Trieste.
Receive expert suggestions for local pairings, ideal for hosting or gifting.

Fashion Boutiques And Designer Stores

High-end Fashion
Trieste has a lot of high-end fashion stores that appeal to customers seeking luxury.
Larusmiani sells upmarket menswear, whereas Vogue Boutique sells trendy women's clothes.

Expect a well chosen range of brand apparel, shoes, and accessories, as well as personalized shopping experiences with personnel to assist you discover the ideal ensemble.

Local Designers
In addition to worldwide labels, Trieste is home to several excellent local designers.
Explore stores like Stella Rossa, where you can find one-of-a-kind objects that capture the city's artistic flair.

Expect unique and exclusive designs, ideal for fashion fans.
Meet designers at exclusive events and trunk presentations.

Vintage and second-hand shops
For those who value sustainable fashion, Trieste features a number of vintage and second-hand boutiques, like Bottega dell'Usato, where you may find pre-owned treasures.

Expect to find unique, one-of-a-kind apparel and accessories at moderate costs, as well as a pleasant shopping ambiance where you may browse vintage findings for hours.

Trieste's shopping environment is a fascinating mix of historic markets, artisan stores, and contemporary boutiques.
Trieste has something for everyone, whether you are looking for one-of-a-kind souvenirs, high-end fashion, or simply enjoying the city's ambiance.

Each street and market reflects the city's personality, making shopping an enjoyable experience rather than a chore.

As you explore, embrace the local culture and do not be afraid to talk to store owners and artists to learn more about the gems you find.

CHAPTER 15

Trieste For Nature Lovers

Trieste is a city that seamlessly combines urban life and breathtaking natural settings, making it an ideal visit for nature enthusiasts.

Those who enjoy the great outdoors will find lots to explore, from the stunning Adriatic coastline to lush parks and large hiking routes.

This chapter will look at the many hiking, biking, birding, and coastline exploring activities available in Trieste.

Hiking And Bike Trails
Nature Trails of the Karst Region
The Karst Region, located only a short drive from Trieste, boasts some of the most spectacular hiking and bike paths in the vicinity.

The Karst, known for its stunning limestone cliffs and distinctive geological formations, is an outdoor enthusiast's heaven.

Key Trails:
Sentiero Rilke: This picturesque trail connects Duino and Sistiana, providing spectacular views of the cliffs and Adriatic Sea.

The track is well-marked and excellent for both walkers and cyclists, leading you through stunning settings teeming with natural vegetation.

Val Rosandra offers trails with varied difficulty levels, making it accessible for anyone.
The region is distinguished by sheer cliffs, gorges, and the flowing Rosandra River, which provide a peaceful environment for trekking and nature trails.

Urban Cycle Routes
For those who like cycling in a more urban setting, Trieste has a network of bike routes that allow you to explore the city while enjoying the green spaces.

Recommended Routes:
The Bici Club Trieste Route offers a fun way to see Trieste's parks and coastline while exercising.

Cycle along the Riva Tre Novembre, a seaside promenade with stunning views of the bay and neighboring hills.

Parks & Gardens
Public Garden Muzio Tommasini
Giardino Pubblico Muzio de Tommasini, located in the city center, is a popular park in Trieste.

With its well-kept gardens, fountains, and statues, it is the perfect place for a leisurely stroll or picnic.

Highlights include beautifully designed gardens with a diverse range of plants and flowers, as well as a tranquil ambiance ideal for relaxation or reading beneath the trees.

The Remembrance Park
Parco della Rimembranza is another green jewel in Trieste, with breathtaking panoramic views of the city and sea.
Locals love running, walking, and spending time outside at the park. Features include scenic walking trails with carefully placed seats for maximum views.

The mix of forested and open areas allows for a variety of outdoor activities.

The Botanical Garden
The Botanical Garden of Trieste is a hidden gem that houses a diverse collection of plant species from throughout the world.

This tranquil location is ideal for nature enthusiasts wishing to immerse themselves in various flora.

Expect:
Well-labeled plants to learn about different species.
Quiet areas and walkways for exploration and introspection.

Bird Watching And Wildlife
Birdwatching Hotspots
Trieste and its neighboring areas provide superb birding possibilities. The different environments span from coastal regions to woodland parks, drawing a variety of bird species all year.

Best Locations:
Laguna di Grado, a coastal lagoon near Trieste, offers excellent birding opportunities.
You may see migrating birds like flamingos, herons, and numerous shorebirds here.

Valerie Rosandra: The valley is ideal not just for trekking but also for seeing birds in their natural environment.

Look for raptors flying overhead, as well as smaller songbirds fluttering among the treetops.

Wildlife Observation
In addition to birds, the region is home to a diverse range of fauna.
Deer, foxes, and a variety of small animals may be found in the natural areas surrounding Trieste.

Tips for Wildlife Watching:
Animals are most active in the early morning or late afternoon, making these the best times to watch them.
Be calm and patient, and bring binoculars to get a better look.

Explore The Adriatic Coastline
Coastal Walks.
The Adriatic shoreline is a beautiful aspect of Trieste, providing amazing vistas and chances for exploration.
The promenade along the shore is ideal for strolling and enjoying the sea breeze.

Popular walking routes:
Molo Audace: Enjoy a leisurely stroll along the long pier that extends into the sea.
You may get panoramic views of the water and the city skyline.

Visit Riva Tre Novembre, a waterfront promenade packed with cafes, for a relaxing stroll or coffee break.

Beaches around Trieste
For those wishing to unwind by the sea, Trieste has various beaches nearby where you may swim, sunbathe, and experience the Mediterranean lifestyle.

Notable beaches include Barcola, which has a lengthy promenade where inhabitants enjoy swimming, sunbathing, and socializing.

The pristine waters and beautiful views of the surrounding hills make it a popular summer destination.

Sistiana Bay, located further out from the city, is a family-friendly beach with calm seas. Swimmers and water sports enthusiasts will love the location.

Watersports
For the more daring nature enthusiasts, the Adriatic Sea provides a variety of water sports activities such as kayaking, paddleboarding, and sailing.

Recommended activities:
Rent a kayak to explore the coastline, including secret coves and beaches.

Sailing Tours: Explore the Adriatic Sea and observe dolphins along the way.

Trieste is a city that values its natural surroundings, making it an excellent choice for environment enthusiasts.
There are many of things to choose from, whether you prefer trekking in the Karst mountains, resting in a park, birding, or visiting the breathtaking Adriatic coastline.

Embrace the outdoors and explore Trieste's magnificent landscapes and dynamic ecosystems.

Whether you are a seasoned explorer or simply want to relax in nature, Trieste is an ideal setting for all of your outdoor activities.

CHAPTER 16

Plan Your Visit to the Beach

Trieste, located on Italy's northeastern edge along the breathtaking Adriatic coastline, is a hidden gem for beach lovers.

While frequently overshadowed by more well-known beach resorts, it has a variety of stunning beaches, lively beach clubs, and water sports.

In this chapter, we will look at Trieste's secret beaches, prominent beach clubs and resorts, interesting water activities, and proper beach etiquette to ensure you have a great day by the sea.

Trieste's Hidden Beaches
Barcola
Barcola, one of Trieste's most popular beaches, spans along the coast and provides a gorgeous setting for sunbathing and swimming.

This beach is very popular with locals, who come here to enjoy the sun during the warmer months.

Highlights:
Barcola provides free beach access, making it a cost-effective option for guests.

The neighboring promenade is ideal for strolling or cycling, with cafes offering cool drinks and gelato options.

Sistiana Bay
Sistiana Bay, a short drive from the city center, with crystal-clear seas and breathtaking views of the surrounding cliffs.

This lovely beach is frequently less crowded than Barcola, making it an excellent choice for those looking for a more relaxing beach experience.

Highlights:
Family-Friendly: The beach is ideal for families, with shallow seas suitable for youngsters.

Sunbeds and umbrellas may be rented, and local eateries provide handy dining options.

Miramare Beach
Located near the old Miramare Castle, this little beach combines natural beauty with historical value.

The beach is located against a backdrop of beautiful gardens and the gorgeous castle, making it an ideal place to unwind.

Highlights:
Enjoy stunning views of the castle and adjacent grounds while relaxing by the sea.

Secluded Atmosphere:
This beach offers a peaceful escape from the masses.

Punta Grossa
For those prepared to travel a little farther, Punta Grossa is a hidden treasure located around 30 minutes from Trieste.

This rocky beach is famous for its breathtaking scenery and pristine seas.

Highlights:
Clear seas near Punta Grossa offer great snorkeling opportunities, allowing you to explore the undersea world.

Natural Beauty: The neighboring cliffs and lush greenery provide a magnificent beach environment.

Popular Beach Clubs And Resorts
Beach Club Trieste
Beach Club Trieste, located on the dynamic Barcola promenade, is a lively venue that offers both rest and enjoyment.
With sun loungers, beach bars, and frequent events, it is an excellent spot to relax and interact.

Features include a cocktail bar where guests may relax in the sun and enjoy a refreshing drink.
The club's many live music events provide a pleasant environment throughout the evenings.

La Perla.
Another popular alternative is La Perla, a beach club that combines comfort and pleasure.
This club, located in Miramare, offers well-kept sunbeds as well as a full-service bar.
La Perla's restaurant offers local seafood and Mediterranean cuisine, ideal for a beachside lunch.

Family-friendly services.
It is an excellent choice for families, featuring features such as children's play areas.

Resort Capo Di Pula
Resort Capo di Pula, located a short drive from Trieste, provides upmarket rooms with private beaches.
It is an excellent alternative for people wishing to indulge in some luxury during their beach vacation.

Features:
The resort offers spa services for a relaxing day of pampering.
The resort offers exclusive beach access for a more personal experience.

Water Sport And Activities
Sail and Boat Tours
The Adriatic Sea is ideal for sailing, and numerous organizations in Trieste provide boat rentals and guided cruises.

Whether you are a seasoned sailor or a beginner, there are alternatives for everyone.

Options:
Day Cruises: Enjoy a relaxed day at sea with organized boat trips that typically stop at scenic coves. Local clubs provide sailing training for novices.

Kayaking and paddleboarding
Exploring the coast by kayak or paddleboard is an excellent opportunity to reconnect with nature and experience Trieste from a new viewpoint.

Rentals are offered at a variety of beaches and water sports facilities.

Benefits:
Kayaking offers access to secret coves and beaches not accessible by land, providing unique views.

Fun for everyone: Individuals and families may enjoy both activities, which provide a wonderful way to spend the day on the lake.

Snorkelling & Diving
Trieste provides great snorkeling and diving possibilities, particularly around Punta Grossa and adjacent coastal regions.

What To Expect:
Explore the vibrant underwater habitats, home to colorful fish and plants.

Local diving schools provide guided dives and courses for all ability levels.

Beach Etiquette & Tips
Respect the environment.
When visiting Trieste's beaches, remember to respect the natural environment.

Avoid littering and remember to take your rubbish with you. Participate in beach cleanups if you come across any organized activities.

Be mindful of personal space
While socializing is enjoyable, keep in mind the amount of space you take up on the beach, particularly in congested locations.

Setting up your towels and belongings with ample space between you and your neighbors allows everyone to relax comfortably.

Swim safely
Pay heed to local swimming rules and weather conditions.
Always swim in specified places and be aware of strong currents.
If you are doubtful, contact lifeguards or locals for help.

Dress appropriately
While swimsuits are appropriate for the beach, consider wearing cover-ups once you leave the sand.
Dressing respectfully to the local culture is appropriate in cafés and stores near the beach.

Respect people when listening to music at the beach.
Use headphones or keep the level down to prevent bothering other beachgoers.

Arrive early
During peak season, attractive beaches may rapidly become congested. Arriving early not only provides you the greatest place, but it also allows you to enjoy the beach in a more peaceful, calm atmosphere.

Trieste is an excellent beach vacation location, with beautiful beaches, lively clubs, and a variety of water sports.

Whether you are looking for secluded coves or relaxing at a beach club, you are sure to find something to your liking.

To have a positive beach experience, remember to respect the environment and adhere to local customs.

Grab your sunscreen, pack your beach gear, and prepare to enjoy Trieste's sun-soaked coastlines!

CHAPTER 17

Family-friendly Activities

Trieste is not just a city rich in history and culture, but it is also an excellent choice for families wishing to make lasting experiences together.

Families may have a well-rounded experience thanks to the many kid-friendly museums, parks, beaches, guided excursions, and neighboring attractions.

In this chapter, we will look at family-friendly activities that are suitable for both younger children and teenagers, ensuring that everyone has fun.

Child-Friendly Museums And Parks

Museo di Storia Naturale

The Natural History Museum in Trieste is a terrific venue for families with children who are interested in the natural world.

The museum has amazing displays on geology, paleontology, and biodiversity. Children may marvel at dinosaur remains while learning about the surrounding flora and animals.

Highlights include interactive exhibits that stimulate hands-on investigation, creating an enjoyable learning experience.

Check the museum's calendar for family programs and kid-friendly activities.

Museo Del Mar
The Maritime Museum is another intriguing choice, particularly for family who enjoy the water.

It focuses on Trieste's rich nautical heritage, which includes shipbuilding, navigation, and ocean exploration.

Features include elaborate model ships and displays about great explorers, which will engage children.

The museum offers educational programs that involve youngsters in maritime-themed activities.

The Remembrance Park
Rimembranza Park is a large green place ideal for a family day out. This park provides plenty of area for youngsters to run, play, and explore.

Family Activities:
Playgrounds provide equipment tailored to different age groups.
Picnic Areas: Enjoy a family meal under the trees.
Family Friendly Beaches And Outdoor Activities

Barcola Beach
Barcola Beach is a family favorite, recognized for its calm seas and lively environment.
It is an ideal spot for families to spend the day by the shore.

Family-Friendly Features:
Shallow water is safe for smaller children to splash and play in.
Beach Activities: Rent paddleboards and kayaks from local beach clubs for a fun day on the sea.

Miramare Park, located next to the stunning Miramare Castle, with wide gardens and lovely pathways.

Families may explore the park's natural splendor while admiring the stunning views of the Adriatic.

Activities for Kids:
Nature Walks: Engage youngsters in a nature treasure hunt as you explore the park.
Explore the castle and its grounds for a cultural and natural experience.

Adventure Parks Trieste has a variety of outdoor adventure parks, including Križ Park.
These parks provide exhilarating experiences for older children and teenagers through ropes courses, zip-lining, and climbing walls.

What To Expect:
Variety of Courses: Suitable for all skill levels. Professional personnel accompany families through activities to ensure their safety and enjoyment.

Guided Tours For Families
Family-Friendly City Tours.
Exploring Trieste on a guided tour is a terrific way to learn about the city's history and culture while keeping the youngsters entertained.

Look for tours designed exclusively for family, which contain entertaining information, games, and interactive activities.

Highlights of some trips include treasure hunts or scavenger hunts, which engage children in exploring the city.

Historical Characters: Guides costumed as historical personalities may enhance the tour experience for youngsters and bring history to life.

Boat Tours
A boat cruise around the Adriatic Sea provides a unique opportunity to observe Trieste from a fresh perspective.
These trips frequently involve landings on surrounding islands and provide an opportunity to learn about marine life.

Family Benefits
Instructive Experience: Boat trips include information about the local ecology, making them both enjoyable and instructive.

Relaxation Time: Taking in the sea wind and scenery may provide a pleasant respite for families on vacation.

Fun Day Trips For Children
Aquileia
Aquileia, an old town just a short drive from Trieste, is well-known for its outstanding archeological treasures.
The remains of a Roman city provide an intriguing look into the past.

Family Activities:
Basilica di Santa Maria Assunta: Explore the beautiful mosaics in this UNESCO World Heritage site.
The Archaeological Museum showcases objects from ancient Rome, captivating youthful minds.

Miramare Castle & Gardens
While not far from Trieste, visiting Miramare Castle might feel like a mini-vacation.
The castle and its adjacent grounds are stunning and offer plenty of area for exploring.

Activities for Families:
The Castle offers family-friendly guided tours with stories to engage children's imaginations.

Why Allow children to explore the gardens and learn about different plant types while enjoying the environment.

The Kocjan Caves
A day excursion to Slovenia's Škocjan Caves provides a memorable journey for families.

This UNESCO World Heritage site has one of the world's biggest subterranean canyons.

What To Expect:
Family-friendly guided tours emphasize the caverns' geological features and are suitable for all ages.

The beautiful structures and subterranean waterways create a fascinating environment, inspiring children's curiosity.

Piran
Piran is a lovely beach village located about an hour from Trieste and is ideal for a day trip.

Its tiny alleys, ancient buildings, and breathtaking beach views make it an enjoyable vacation.

Family-Friendly Features:
Piran's calm waters make it ideal for swimming.
Visit Tartini Square, named for renowned musician Giuseppe Tartini, to learn about the town's rich history and cultural heritage.

Trieste is an excellent family vacation location, with a wide range of activities suitable for all ages.

There is plenty of fun to be had whether you are visiting kid-friendly museums, going on outdoor excursions, or taking guided tours.

Trieste's combination of culture, beauty, and excitement will undoubtedly leave a lasting impression on families visiting this magnificent Italian city.

So pack your luggage, collect the kids, and prepare for a family adventure in Trieste!

CHAPTER 18

Romantic Activities to Do in Trieste

Trieste, with its breathtaking seaside vistas, beautiful neighborhoods, and rich cultural past, is a romantic destination for couples.

Whether you are celebrating an anniversary, planning a honeymoon, or simply looking for a romantic trip, this city has several options to make wonderful memories.

In this chapter, we will look at the most romantic things Trieste has to offer, from gorgeous sunset views to wonderful dining experiences and tranquil spa getaways.

Sunset Spots
Piazza Unità d'Italia
Begin your romantic evening at Piazza Unità d'Italia, one of Europe's largest beachfront squares.

As the sun sets, the plaza changes into a spectacular spectacle, with the golden hues of evening illuminating the wonderful buildings.

Why It is Romantic:
The magnificent views of the Adriatic Sea provide for a lovely setting.

Take a leisurely stroll across the area and stop at a café or gelato shop to enjoy local sweets while admiring the scenery.

Miramare Castle Garden
The gardens around Miramare Castle provide an ideal location for couples.
As the sun sets behind the castle, the gardens transform into a beautiful paradise, ideal for a romantic stroll.

Highlights:
Enjoy lush foliage and blossoming flowers along scenic paths.
Find a quiet seat overlooking the water to enjoy the sunset together.

Barcola Promenade
The Barcola Promenade is another great site to see the sunset.

This seaside path is adorned with palm palms and seats, making it ideal for a romantic evening stroll.

Enjoy the gentle sea wind while walking hand-in-hand along the coast.

Seek out calmer locations to relax and enjoy the soothing sound of the waves.

Romantic Dinners With Wine Tasting
Fine Dining Restaurants.
Trieste has various fine dining establishments that offer an ideal setting for a romantic supper.

Consider arranging a seat at Ristorante Al Bagatto, which is famed for its delicious Italian cuisine and sophisticated atmosphere.

Dining Experience:
Experience an intimate environment with illuminated tables and exceptional service.
Enjoy delicious local cuisine and wine pairings.

Wine tasting in the Collio region.
The Collio wine area, located just a short drive from Trieste, is renowned for its white wines and picturesque vineyards.

Book a wine-tasting trip for an unforgettable experience.

What to Expect:
Tour scenic vineyards and learn about the winemaking process.

Tastings with a View: Pair local cheeses and meats with breathtaking views of the rolling hills.

Romantic Wine Bars
For a more informal yet personal evening, head to one of Trieste's beautiful wine bars, such as Caffè degli Specchi.
In this pleasant setting, you may try a selection of local wines.

Why It is Ideal:
Select from a wide range of local wines, including well-known whites. The soft lighting and small chairs provide a cozy atmosphere ideal for sharing a drink and conversation.

Couples Spa Retreats
Spa in the Savoia Excelsior Palace Hotel
A couples' treatment at the Spa at the Savoia Excelsior Palace Hotel is a luxury pampering experience.

This five-star hotel provides a variety of spa services aimed to promote relaxation and regeneration.

Spa Features:
Couples massages: Enjoy a peaceful massage tailored for two, allowing you to unwind together.

Personalized Wellness Treatments: Choose from facials and body cleanses to meet your specific needs.

Roman Terme
Terme di Romanèe, located just outside of Trieste, is a well-known thermal spa that provides a relaxing vacation for couples.
Immerse yourself in natural hot springs and receive a range of health treatments.

What to do:
Relax in warm thermal pools surrounded by lush plants.
Consider spa packages that include massages, body treatments, and access to wellness facilities.

Scenic Walks And Boat Rides

Walk along the Canal Grande.
The Canal Grande in Trieste provides a stunning backdrop for a romantic stroll.

This attractive neighborhood is dotted with colorful houses and cafés, which creates a lovely ambiance.

Highlights:
Cross the picturesque bridges and admire the reflections on the river while walking.

Cafés on the Canal: Enjoy a coffee or aperitivo while watching the world go by.
Boat ride on the Adriatic Sea
Consider going on a boat cruise around the Adriatic coast.

Many operators provide short trips that allow you to see the beauty of the water from a new angle.
Expect magnificent views of Trieste from the sea, including the gorgeous shoreline and neighboring hills.

Relaxing atmosphere: Enjoy the gentle sway of the boat while admiring the beauty of the Adriatic.

Hike the Strada Napoleonica
For couples who appreciate outdoor activities, trekking the Strada Napoleonica provides both adventure and breathtaking scenery.

This ancient walkway follows the cliffs, offering panoramic views of the Gulf of Trieste.

Why It is Romantic:
Natural beauty: This trek offers a peaceful retreat from city life.
Picnic Spots: Enjoy a lunch at a picturesque overlook with amazing views.

Go to Velika Plaža

For a beach day, visit Velika Plaža, which is located just outside of Trieste. This vast stretch of beach is ideal for a day of leisure.

Activities:

Sunbathing and swimming: Enjoy the sun and cool down in the pristine waters.
Beachfront restaurants provide fresh seafood and local delicacies, ideal for a romantic lunch or dinner by the sea.

Trieste offers a plethora of romantic adventures, including magnificent sunsets, intimate dinners, peaceful spa getaways, and picturesque walks.

Whether you are enjoying a glass of local wine or strolling through the picturesque streets with your loved one, Trieste has limitless opportunity to make memorable memories.

So pack your luggage and prepare for a romantic journey in this enchanting city!

The Trieste Equilibrium

Where Central Europe leans gently into the Mediterranean, and history lingers like sea mist over cobbled streets. Here, coffee isn't rushed, the wind carries forgotten poems, and life finds balance between cultures, coastlines, and quiet moments of wonder.

CHAPTER 19

Hidden Gems of Trieste

While Trieste is well-known for its magnificent piazzas and prominent sights, there are still many hidden gems waiting to be found.

For those prepared to venture beyond the conventional tourist trails, this city provides one-of-a-kind encounters that show its genuine appeal.

This chapter will reveal off-the-beaten-path sights, lesser-known historical places, small local cafés, hidden restaurants, and secret settings ideal for photographers.

Off-Beaten-Path Attractions

Museum of Reorganization

The Museo del Risorgimento, located in the center of Trieste, is dedicated to the history of Italian unification.

This little museum may not be on every tourist's itinerary, but it offers an intriguing peek into a watershed moment in Italian history.

Why Visit:
Intimate Experience: With fewer people, visitors may examine the exhibits at their own speed and learn about the rich historical backdrop.

The museum's engaging exhibits, including relics, papers, and multimedia displays, vividly depict Italy's unification.

San Giusto Hill offers a panoramic view of the city. While many people rush to the more famous Miramare Castle, San Giusto provides a more tranquil experience with beautiful views.

What To Expect:
Visit St. Giusto Cathedral, set on a hill, for exquisite mosaics and a quiet environment.
Explore the remnants of the old Roman theater and fortress, which provide a concrete link to Trieste's history.

Museum of the History of Fumetto
Comic book fans will like the Museum of Comic Art, a hidden gem that embraces the world of comics and graphic novels.
This unique museum displays both Italian and foreign comic art.

Highlights:
The museum's rotating exhibits spotlight diverse artists and genres, keeping the experience fresh and fascinating.

Interactive areas: Interact with the art through interactive exhibits and courses tailored to both children and adults.

Lesser-known Historical Sites
The Jewish Museum in Trieste
The Jewish Museum provides an in-depth look at Trieste's Jewish community history.

This lesser-known institution is not only informative, but also demonstrates the city's vast cultural variety.

Why This Matters:
The museum's collection of religious objects, papers, and pictures chronicles Jewish life in Trieste.

The museum conducts lectures and cultural activities that highlight Jewish traditions and contributions to Trieste.

The Arco Di Riccardo
The Arco di Riccardo, a beautiful Roman arch in the ancient town, is often ignored.

This ancient edifice, dating from the first century BC, is an important part of Trieste's architectural legacy.

Visit for:
Historical significance.
It is one of the few surviving examples of Roman architecture in the city.

Quiet surroundings: Enjoy the serene atmosphere as you admire this historic relic away from the crowded tourist attractions.

Church of San Niccolò
Chiesa di San Nicolò, a hidden gem, with spectacular baroque architecture and interiors.

Often overlooked by visitors, it provides a peaceful sanctuary for anyone looking to discover Trieste's spiritual side.

Why It is Special:
The church boasts intricate paintings and art, which are typically ignored in guidebooks.

Enjoy a peaceful atmosphere away from people and see the stunning architecture.

Why It is Special:
The church boasts intricate paintings and art, which are typically ignored in guidebooks.

Enjoy a peaceful atmosphere away from people and see the stunning architecture.

Why it is Worth a Visit:
Historical Charm: The café has housed many prominent personalities, including writers and painters, making it a living history.

Try their classic pastries, which combine well with coffee.

Osteria de Marino
Osteria da Marino, a secret restaurant, is noted for its traditional Triestine cuisine and welcoming setting.

It is popular among residents since it is remote from the main tourist attractions.

Expect to enjoy handcrafted cuisine produced using fresh, local ingredients.
comfortable, rustic décor makes for a welcome environment for romantic dinners or informal meals with friends.

Antico Caffe Pasticceria
Antico Caffè Pasticceria is a must-visit for individuals who enjoy sweets. This tiny café serves handcrafted sweets and pastries in a pleasant environment.

Highlights:
Artisan Treats: Try traditional delicacies like strudel and local pastries. The café's charming design and ambiance make it a great place to relax after touring.
Secret Spots For Photographers

The Old Port (Porto Vecchio)
The Old Port region is a photographer's dream, capturing the rocky beauty of Trieste's shoreline as well as its ancient buildings.
This often-overlooked location offers interesting photographic opportunities.

Photographic Tips:
Visit around sunrise or sunset to see spectacular lighting that enhances the landscape's splendor.

Industrial Charm: Photograph the contrast between antique port architecture and the calm Adriatic seas.

Miramare Park's Hidden Corners
While many people visit Miramare Castle, the adjoining Miramare Park contains lesser-known spots ideal for taking spectacular nature photos.

What To Look For:
Explore the park's pathways to discover isolated areas with stunning views of the sea and gardens.
Capture local wildlife with your camera, including birds and plants.

Via Delle Torri
Via delle Torri, a lovely street dotted with attractive homes, provides a look into the gentler side of Trieste.
It is ideal for capturing the spirit of city life.

Why it is Ideal for Photography:
Capture authentic scenes of villagers going about their day in this serene area.
The colorful facades stand out against the blue sky, creating breathtaking pictures.

The Botanical Garden in Trieste
The Botanical Garden is a hidden gem for nature enthusiasts and photographers alike.
This tranquil oasis boasts a broad range of plant species, providing a colorful backdrop for photographs.

Photography highlights include capturing the magnificence of exotic plants and flowers in bloom year-round.

Quiet Retreat: Enjoy uninterrupted nature photography in a peaceful setting.
Exploring Trieste's hidden treasures allows you to experience the city as a native, discovering unique stories and lesser-known sites.

Trieste has a multitude of experiences that will enrich your vacation and leave you with lasting memories, from calm historical places and comfortable cafés to secret settings for breathtaking photography.

So, venture off the usual road and discover the charming mysteries that await you in this stunning Italian city.

CHAPTER 20

Practical Advice for Longer Stays

When planning a longer stay in Trieste, whether for job, school, or vacation, comprehending the local terrain is critical.

This chapter will provide you practical guidance on how to rent an apartment, navigate food shopping, connect with expats, and deal with paperwork and bureaucracy.

Each component is intended to assist you transition into your new surroundings with ease and confidence.

Rental Apartments In Trieste

Finding the Right Apartment

Renting an apartment in Trieste might provide a more genuine experience than staying at a hotel.

You will be able to live like a local while still enjoying additional room and facilities.
Consider online platforms such as Airbnb and Booking.com, as well as local ads like Subito.

It can help you locate both short-term and long-term rentals.
Facebook groups for expats in Trieste routinely publish available flats.

Consult with local real estate agents specializing in rentals.

They can assist you explore the market and identify houses that match your needs.

Different types of rentals

You can discover a variety of possibilities, from modern flats in the city center to charming residences in calmer districts.

Consider your lifestyle choices and budget.

When choosing a location, prioritize proximity to public transportation, food shops, and job or school.

Neighborhoods like San Giacomo and Barriera Vecchia have a more local feel, but the city center is more lively and tourist-friendly.

Look for basic amenities such as a fully outfitted kitchen, laundry facilities, and Wi-Fi.

Consider whether you require parking or other special amenities.

Lease Terms and Conditions.
Before signing a lease, be sure you understand the terms and conditions.

Key Points:
Confirm lease duration and flexibility. Some landlords may provide month-to-month choices.

Prepare to pay a security deposit, usually one or two months' rent.

Clarify the utilities included in the rent (e.g., water, electricity, internet) and your duties.

Grocery And Local Markets Shopping for essentials
Knowing where to buy for food will make your stay much more pleasant.

Trieste has a combination of sophisticated supermarkets and beautiful local markets.

Trieste's major supermarkets, Coop and Conad, provide a diverse range of food, home supplies, and personal care products.

Eurospin offers budget-friendly solutions, particularly for everyday needs.

Local Markets
Exploring local markets is not only a good method to get fresh fruit, but it is also a fun cultural experience.

Recommended markets include Mercato Coperto, which offers fresh produce, meat, and local specialties.
Visiting on a Saturday morning yields the freshest selection.

Piazza San Giovanni is a modest and picturesque market where local sellers offer seasonal fruits, vegetables, and handcrafted crafts.

It is ideal for a leisurely walk while picking up fresh produce.

Tips for Shopping
Know your labels: Familiarize yourself with Italian brands, particularly for everyday things. For example, "latte" denotes milk, whereas "pane" indicates bread.

Cash and cards: Although most establishments accept credit cards, certain local marketplaces may prefer cash, particularly for minor transactions.
It is a good idea to keep some euros on hand for such times.

Networking And Meeting With Expats
Connecting with the Community.
Creating a network of friends and acquaintances will help you enjoy your time in Trieste.
Engaging with the local expat community may bring both support and friendship.

How to meet expats:
Join Trieste-specific expat Facebook groups.
These are ideal for exchanging experiences, asking questions, and discovering social activities.

Meetup.com hosts events for a variety of hobbies, including hiking, language exchange, and eating.
These events are ideal for meeting others who share your interests.

Language courses: Taking an Italian language class not only helps you learn the language, but also connects you with other students, many of whom are expats.

Local clubs and organizations.
Consider joining a local club or group to broaden your network.

Options include:
Cultural Associations: Search for clubs that promote cultural interaction.
They frequently host events where you can learn about local traditions while also meeting new people.

Joining a local sports team might help you meet new people and keep active.
Trieste offers soccer, jogging, and cycling groups, among other activities.

Working With Paperwork And Bureaucracy
Understanding the Local Regulations
Navigating the bureaucratic landscape may be difficult, particularly in a foreign nation.

Understanding the required papers and local rules is critical for a successful stay.

Key Documents:
If you want to stay for more than 90 days, you may need to register your residency with the local municipality (Comune).
Check the official website for specific requirements.

Get health insurance that covers your stay in Italy.
If you want to remain for a lengthy amount of time, you might consider enrolling with Italy's National Health Service (Servizio Sanitario Nazionale).

Setting Up Utilities
If you are renting an apartment, you will probably need to set up utilities such as electricity, gas, and internet.

Steps To Follow:
Contact providers: Look at local providers and contact them to set up your accounts.
Major corporations such as Enel provide energy and gas, while a variety of companies provide internet services.
Be prepared to present identity and proof of residence when setting up utilities.

Navigating the Italian bureaucracy
Dealing with Italian bureaucracy can be difficult, but knowing the system will assist.

Tips for Success:
Patience is key.
Italian bureaucracy may be sluggish, so patience is required.
If you have not heard back about your applications or requests, be sure to follow up.

Consider hiring a local expert or firm for specialized paperwork, such as visas and residency permits, if feeling overwhelmed.

By planning ahead of time and following these practical advice, you may make your longer stay in Trieste productive and pleasurable.

From choosing the ideal apartment and engaging with locals to navigating the bureaucratic landscape, this chapter will provide you with the knowledge you need to survive in this dynamic Italian city.

APPENDIX

This chapter serves as a comprehensive resource for travelers to Trieste, providing essential emergency contacts, navigational tools, recommended readings, useful local phrases, and locations of tourism centers.

Having this information readily available can enhance your experience in the city, ensuring that you are well-prepared for any situation.

Emergency Contacts
Knowing how to reach local authorities and emergency services is crucial when traveling. Here are the key emergency contacts you should keep on hand during your stay in Trieste:

Emergency Services

General Emergency (Police, Fire, Ambulance): Dial 112
Police Station:
Polizia di Stato: +39 040 379 2111
Address: Via della Madonna del Mare, 10, 34123 Trieste TS, Italy.

Medical Emergencies
Emergency Medical Services: Dial 118
Local Hospitals:
Ospedale di Cattinara: +39 040 399 5111
Address: Via Cattinara, 25, 34149 Trieste TS, Italy.
Ospedale Maggiore: +39 040 399 5111
Address: Via Duca d'Aosta, 1, 34129 Trieste TS, Italy.

Fire Department
Fire Services: Dial 115
Local Fire Station:
Comando Provinciale dei Vigili del Fuoco di Trieste: +39 040 377 3111
Address: Via Francesco Crispi, 1, 34124 Trieste TS, Italy.

Poison Control
National Poison Control Center: +39 02 661 01029

Maps and Navigational Tools
Navigating a new city can be daunting, but there are various resources to help you get around Trieste effectively.

Offline Maps
Maps.me: This app allows you to download maps for offline use. Great for navigating without mobile data.
CityMaps2Go: A free app that offers offline maps and the ability to save locations and routes.

Online Maps
Google Maps: A reliable resource for finding locations, public transport routes, and more. Accessible at www.google.com/maps.
OpenStreetMap: A collaborative mapping project that provides detailed maps, which can be found at www.openstreetmap.org.

Tourist Information Maps
Upon arrival, pick up a free tourist map at local tourism centers. These maps often include key attractions, public transport routes, and local tips.

Additional Reading And References

For those interested in diving deeper into Trieste's history, culture, and attractions, consider the following readings:

Books
"Trieste: A Cultural History" by Nicky Gardner: This book delves into the rich history and cultural significance of Trieste, offering insight into its multifaceted identity.

"The Comfort of Things" by Iain Sinclair: This work explores the physical and emotional landscape of Trieste, providing a unique perspective on the city.

Online Resources
Visit Trieste: The official tourism website provides extensive information about attractions, events, and practical tips.
Visit at www.triestetourism.it.

Cultural Institute of Trieste: Offers resources on local cultural events, history, and exhibitions. Find it at www.culturaitaliana.it.

Useful Local Phrases
Familiarizing yourself with basic Italian phrases can enhance your interactions and experiences in Trieste.
Here are some useful expressions:

Basic Greetings
Hello: Ciao
Good Morning: Buongiorno
Good Evening: Buonasera
Good Night: Buonanotte

Common Phrases
Thank You: Grazie
Please: Per favore
Excuse Me / Sorry: Scusa / Mi scusi
Yes: Sì
No: No

Directions
Where is...?: Dov'è...?
How do I get to...?: Come arrivo a...?
Left: Sinistra
Right: Destra
Straight Ahead: Dritto

Dining
Menu: Menu
The Bill, please: Il conto, per favore
Delicious: Delizioso

Tourism Centers and Locations
Trieste has several tourism centers that can provide valuable information and resources to enhance your visit.

These centers often have brochures, maps, and knowledgeable staff who can assist with your inquiries.

Main Tourism Office
Trieste Tourist Information Center
Address: Piazza Unità d'Italia, 4, 34121 Trieste TS, Italy.
Phone: +39 040 676 1234
Website: www.triestetourism.it

Other Useful Locations
Castello di Miramare Visitor Center
Address: Viale Miramare, 34151 Trieste TS, Italy.
Phone: +39 040 224 143
Website: www.miramare.beniculturali.it

Museo Revoltella
Address: Via di Revoltella, 14, 34151 Trieste TS, Italy.
Phone: +39 040 675 4050
Website: www.museorevoltella.it

Aquarium of Trieste
Address: Riva Nazario Sauro, 1, 34121 Trieste TS, Italy.
Phone: +39 040 573 0287
Website: www.acquarioditrieste.it

Addresses And Locations Of Popular Accommodation

Finding the right place to stay is crucial for a memorable trip. Here are some popular accommodations in Trieste:

Luxury Resorts
Savoia Excelsior Palace
Address: Riva del Mandracchio, 4, 34124 Trieste TS, Italy.
Website: www.savoiaexcelsiorpalace.com

Hotel Excelsior
Address: Viale Miramare, 16, 34136 Trieste TS, Italy.
Website: www.hotelexcelsiortrieste.com

Mid-Range Hotels
Hotel Continentale
Address: Corso Cavour, 7, 34132 Trieste TS, Italy.
Website: www.hotelcontinentale.com

Hotel Italia
Address: Via Giulia, 81, 34121 Trieste TS, Italy.
Website: www.hotelitaliatrieste.com

Budget-Friendly Options
Hotel Alabarda
Address: Via Alabarda, 12, 34121 Trieste TS, Italy.
Website: www.hotelalabarda.com

Youth Hostel Trieste
Address: Via delle Borse, 4, 34121 Trieste TS, Italy.
Website: www.yhtrieste.com

Unique Stays
Hostel L'Angolo
Address: Via della Ferrovia, 4, 34132 Trieste TS, Italy.
Website: www.hostellangelo.com

Villa Bottini
Address: Via delle Orfane, 5, 34127 Trieste TS, Italy.
Website: www.villabottini.com

Addresses And Locations Of Popular Restaurants And Cafés
Trieste is a culinary delight, offering a mix of traditional and contemporary dining options.
Here are some top restaurants and cafés:

Traditional Restaurants
Trattoria da Lino
Address: Via del Monte, 5, 34124 Trieste TS, Italy.
Website: www.trattoriadalino.com

Ristorante Al Bagatto
Address: Via Monte Grappa, 8, 34131 Trieste TS, Italy.
Website: www.albagatto.com

Contemporary Dining
Osteria Da Marino
Address: Via Duca d'Aosta, 20, 34129 Trieste TS, Italy.
Website: www.osteriadamarino.com

Ristorante Da Giovanni
Address: Riva Nazario Sauro, 2, 34121 Trieste TS, Italy.
Website: www.dagiovanni.com

Cafés
Caffè San Marco
Address: Via Cesare Battisti, 18, 34125 Trieste TS, Italy.
Website: www.caffesanmarco.com

Pasticceria Pivato
Address: Via Giuseppe Mazzini, 17, 34121 Trieste TS, Italy.
Website: www.pasticceriapivato.com

Addresses And Locations Of Popular Bars And Clubs

For those looking to enjoy the nightlife in Trieste, here are some recommended bars and clubs:

Bars
Bar Stella
Address: Via S. Caterina, 1, 34126 Trieste TS, Italy.
Website: www.barstella.com

Caffè degli Specchi
Address: Piazza Unità d'Italia, 7, 34121 Trieste TS, Italy.
Website: www.caffedeglispecchi.com

Nightclubs
Mikado Club
Address: Via R. M. Arnaldi, 12, 34135 Trieste TS, Italy.
Website: www.mikadoclub.com

Club 25
Address: Via Roma, 25, 34132 Trieste TS, Italy.
Website: www.club25trieste.com

Addresses And Locations Of Top Attractions

Trieste boasts a variety of attractions, from historical landmarks to natural wonders. Here are some must-visit sites:

Historical Sites
Piazza Unità d'Italia
Address: Piazza Unità d'Italia, 34121 Trieste TS, Italy.
Website: www.turismofvg.it

Miramare Castle
Address: Viale Miramare, 34151 Trieste TS, Italy.
Website: www.miramare.beniculturali.it

Museums and Galleries
Museo Revoltella
Address: Via di Revoltella, 14, 34151 Trieste TS, Italy.
Website: www.museorevoltella.it

Museo Teatrale Carlo Schmidl
Address: Via A. Diaz, 5, 34124 Trieste TS, Italy.
Website: www.museoteatrale.it

Natural Attractions
Val Rosandra Nature Reserve
Address: Località Bagnoli della Rosandra, 34100 Trieste TS, Italy.
Website: www.parks.it

Vittoria Light (Faro della Vittoria)
Address: Via dell'Istria, 2, 34126 Trieste TS, Italy.
Website: www.farodellavittoria.it

Addresses And Locations Of Bookshops

For book lovers, Trieste has charming bookstores worth visiting:
Local Bookstores
Libreria Antiquaria Pizzicato
Address: Via C. Battisti, 3, 34125 Trieste TS, Italy.
Website: www.pizzicato.it

Libreria Moderna
Address: Via S. Nicolò, 4, 34121 Trieste TS, Italy.
Website: www.libreriamoderna.com

English Bookstores
Bookshop in Trieste
Address: Via dei Capitelli, 3, 34121 Trieste TS, Italy.
Website: www.bookshoptrieste.com

Addresses And Locations Of Top Clinics, Hospitals, And Pharmacies

Staying healthy while traveling is essential. Here are some top medical facilities in Trieste:

Bospitals
Ospedale di Cattinara
Address: Via Cattinara, 25, 34149 Trieste TS, Italy.
Website: www.asuits.sanita.fvg.it

Ospedale Maggiore
Address: Via Duca d'Aosta, 1, 34129 Trieste TS, Italy.
Website: www.ospedale-maggiore.trieste.it

Pharmacies
Farmacia Centrale
Address: Via R. G. R. R. di Trieste, 21, 34121 Trieste TS, Italy.
Website: www.farmaciacentrale.it

Farmacia del Teatro
Address: Via A. Diaz, 7, 34124 Trieste TS, Italy.
Website: www.farmaciadelteatro.it

Addresses And Locations Of UNESCO World Heritage Sites
Trieste is near several UNESCO World Heritage Sites that are worth exploring:

Early Christian Monuments of Ravenna
Location: Ravenna, approximately 150 km from Trieste.
Website: www.ravenna-tourism.it

Venetian Works of Defence
Location: Various locations in Veneto, including cities like Venice and Vicenza.
Website: www.visitveneto.com

The City of Verona
Location: Verona, approximately 120 km from Trieste.
Website: www.tourism.verona.it

This appendix serves as a vital resource for navigating your visit to Trieste, providing essential addresses for accommodation, dining, nightlife, attractions, bookstores, medical facilities, and UNESCO World Heritage Sites.

With this information, you can ensure a well-rounded and enjoyable experience in this beautiful Italian city. Happy exploring!

MAP OF TRIESTE

SCAN QR CODE USING YOUR PHONE
TO ACCESS LIVE MAPS

VISIT HTTPS://TINYURL.COM/46VB5XKD

MAP OF TRIEST STREET

SCAN QR CODE USING YOUR PHONE
TO ACCESS LIVE MAPS

VISIT HTTPS://TINYURL.COM/4H62BDM4

TRIESTE PROVINCE MAP

SCAN QR CODE USING YOUR PHONE
TO ACCESS LIVE MAPS

VISIT   HTTPS://TINYURL.COM/4H62BDM4

TRIESTE OSM

SCAN QR CODE USING YOUR PHONE
TO ACCESS LIVE MAPS

VISIT   HTTPS://TINYURL.COM/4H62BDM4

MAP OF TRIESTE

SCAN QR CODE USING YOUR PHONE
TO ACCESS LIVE MAPS

VISIT HTTPS://TINYURL.COM/47SACWZP

MUSEUMS IN TRIESTE

SCAN QR CODE USING YOUR PHONE
TO ACCESS LIVE MAPS

VISIT   HTTPS://TINYURL.COM/3T4PK22Z

THINGS TO DO IN TRIESTE

SCAN QR CODE USING YOUR PHONE
TO ACCESS LIVE MAPS

VISIT   HTTPS://TINYURL.COM/2S4AWH3D

RESTAURANTS IN TRIESTE

SCAN QR CODE USING YOUR PHONE
TO ACCESS LIVE MAPS

VISIT HTTPS://TINYURL.COM/3X2U227E

References & Accreditions

hhttps://pixabay.com/photos/trieste-bronze-seagull-sculpture-3480172/ https://pixabay.com/photos/silhouette-person-rushing-terminal-4796573/ https://pixabay.com/photos/trieste-italy-friuli-capital-city-174719/ https://pixabay.com/photos/trieste-italy-friuli-capital-city-174719/ https://pixabay.com/photos/gondola-venice-italy-canal-2092617/ https://pixabay.com/photos/venezia-flixbus-ferry-bus-italy-4736523/ https://pixabay.com/photos/helicopter-italy-trieste-control-273273/ https://pixabay.com/photos/lake-garda-ferry-italy-boat-lake-6587095/ https://pixabay.com/photos/port-ferry-cars-italy-ancona-wait-319316/

https://pixabay.com/photos/best-pleasure-the-dolomites-pass-5046132/ https://pixabay.com/photos/pisa-leaning-tower-of-pisa-4420684/ https://pixabay.com/photos/castle-italy-trieste-architecture-4357444/ https://pixabay.com/photos/castle-italy-trieste-architecture-4357444/ https://pixabay.com/photos/venice-grand-canal-sunset-italy-6489813/

https://pixabay.com/photos/museum-history-tourism-architecture-4077339/ https://pixabay.com/photos/cathedral-building-architecture-1066314/ https://pixabay.com/photos/mill-windmill-scoop-mill-4501365/ https://pixabay.com/photos/museum-artwork-colorful-painting-8929637/ https://pixabay.com/photos/italy-trieste-city-architecture-4511398/ https://pixabay.com/photos/light-house-lighthouse-white-blue-314287/

https://pixabay.com/photos/synagogue-judaism-jews-faith-7385636/ https://commons.wikimedia.org/wiki/File:Vista_Panoramica_con_Faro_della_Vittoria.jpg

https://pixabay.com/photos/miramare-castle-trieste-italy-2711856/ https://pixabay.com/photos/port-city-ships-italy-porto-ercole-226515/ https://pixabay.com/photos/nature-travel-exploration-valley-6638062/ https://pixabay.com/photos/port-old-trieste-italy-white-1803344/ https://pixabay.com/photos/colorful-houses-canal-channel-5767937/

References & Accreditions

https://pixabay.com/photos/pizza-food-italy-3000273/
https://pixabay.com/photos/meatball-ravioli-italian-food-964959/
https://pixabay.com/photos/coffee-coffee-break-coffe-break-3689529/
https://pixabay.com/photos/coffe-olde-boy-2269724/
https://pixabay.com/photos/mountains-nature-tourism-hike-6486093/
https://pixabay.com/photos/decoration-ad-light-lights-guitar-4818152/

https://pixabay.com/photos/balderschwang-alps-hut-restaurant-447187/
https://pixabay.com/photos/notebook-camera-map-pencil-travel-1130742/
https://pixabay.com/photos/hat-crafts-art-tradition-culture-6801736/
https://pixabay.com/photos/city-night-birds-eye-view-5644601/

https://pixabay.com/photos/drink-glass-pouring-bar-pub-ice-1870139/
https://pixabay.com/photos/club-bar-music-light-people-378021/
https://pixabay.com/photos/happy-holidays-woman-shopping-3040029/
https://pixabay.com/photos/sea-trieste-italy-boat-nature-7391990/

https://pixabay.com/photos/european-bee-eater-birds-animals-9030680/
https://pixabay.com/photos/family-game-fun-outdoors-playing-4477874/

https://pixabay.com/photos/children-teenagers-walking-running-9608394/
https://pixabay.com/photos/couple-love-romance-man-woman-7088022/
https://pixabay.com/photos/standup-paddleboarding-paddle-board-6342951/

https://pixabay.com/photos/apartment-to-sell-landlord-sold-743378/
https://pixabay.com/photos/real-estate-homeownership-homebuying-6688945/

References & Accreditions

https://commons.wikimedia.org/wiki/File:Trieste_strade.PNG https://commons.wikimedia.org/wiki/File:Trieste-province-map.PNG#/media/File:Trieste-province-map.PNG https://commons.wikimedia.org/w/index.php?search=map+of+trieste&title=Special%3AMediaSearch&type=image https://commons.wikimedia.org/w/index.php?search=map+of+trieste&title=Special%3AMediaSearch&type=image

https://www.google.com/maps/search/museums+in+Trieste/@45.6477502,13.7724879,15.85z?entry=ttu&g_ep=EgoyMDI1MDYxMC4xIKXMDSoASAFQAw%3D%3D

https://www.google.com/maps/place/Trieste,+Province+of+Trieste,+Italy/@45.6523451,13.6360088,12z/data=!3m1!4b1!4m6!3m5!1s0x477b6b06e4edf533:0x666a2484d4dd2b50!8m2!3d45.6508342!4d13.7674486!16zL20vMGZqc2w?entry=ttu&g_ep=EgoyMDI1MDYxMS4wIKXMDSoASAFQAw%3D%3D

https://www.google.com/maps/search/restaurants+in+Trieste/@45.649562,13.773223,15.58z?entry=ttu&g_ep=EgoyMDI1MDYxMS4wIKXMDSoASAFQAw%3D%3D

https://www.google.com/maps/search/things+to+do++in+Trieste/@45.6468436,13.7910702,14.38z?entry=ttu&g_ep=EgoyMDI1MDYxMC4xIKXMDSoASAFQAw%3D%3D

https://commons.wikimedia.org/wiki/File:Cesare_Dell%27Acqua_-_La_proclamazione_del_Portofranco_di_Trieste_-_Inv.5_-_Revoltella_Museum.jpg#/media/File:Cesare_Dell'Acqua_-_La_proclamazione_del_Portofranco_di_Trieste_-_Inv.5_-_Revoltella_Museum.jpg

https://pixabay.com/photos/trieste-italy-mountains-106869/ (cover page)